MW00830546

KNOWING
WHO WE ARE

KNOWING WHO WE ARE
The Wesleyan Way of Grace

Knowing Who We Are
978-1-7910-3203-6
978-1-7910-3202-9 eBook

Knowing Who We Are: Leader Guide
978-1-7910-3205-0
978-1-7910-3204-3 eBook

Knowing Who We Are: DVD
978-1-7910-3206-7

Who We Are And What We Believe:
50 Questions about The UMC
(a companion reader to the study)
978-1-7910-3208-1
978-1-7910-3207-4 eBook

Also by Laceye C. Warner

All the Good:
A Wesleyan Way of Christmas

The Method of Our Mission:
United Methodist Polity & Organization

Laceye C. Warner

KNOWING WHO WE ARE

The Wesleyan Way of Grace

WHAT WE BELIEVE, WHAT WE DO, AND WHY

Abingdon Press | Nashville

Knowing Who We Are:

The Wesleyan Way of Grace

Copyright © 2024 Abingdon Press
All rights reserved.

No part of this work may be reproduced or transmitted in any form or by any means, electronic or mechanical, including photocopying and recording, or by any information storage or retrieval system, except as may be expressly permitted by the 1976 Copyright Act, the 1998 Digital Millennium Copyright Act, or in writing from the publisher. Requests for permission can be addressed to Rights and Permissions, The United Methodist Publishing House, 810 12th Avenue South, Nashville, TN 37203-4704 or emailed to permissions@abingdonpress.com.

Library of Congress Control Number: 2024931193
978-1-7910-3203-6

Scripture quotations are from the New Revised Standard Version, Updated Edition. Copyright © 2021 National Council of Churches of Christ in the United States of America. Used by permission. All rights reserved worldwide.

Text quotations for the *The Sermons of John Wesley* are taken from the 1872 edition edited by Thomas Jackson. A complete listing of the text of the sermons can be found at https://www.resourceumc.org/en/topics /history/john-wesley-sermons/title-index.

MANUFACTURED IN THE UNITED STATES OF AMERICA

CONTENTS

INTRODUCTION
KNOWING WHO WE ARE

"Who is a Methodist?" and "what is the mark?"
John Wesley, "The Character of a Methodist," 1742

These questions and their response were written by John Wesley, the founder and leader of early Methodism, as part of a booklet composed in response to criticisms he received in the earliest years of the movement. Though Methodism persists centuries later, we still reflect on our identity and purpose, sometimes in response to criticisms, to remember who we were, who we are, and who we want to be. Even centuries later, we continue to resonate with the roots of Methodism established by John and Charles Wesley, the founders of the early Methodist renewal movement. With the earliest Methodists we recognize the mark, or main characteristic, of Methodism is grounded in love. Love of God that connects to love of neighbors. John Wesley responded to the questions above with the following statement: "A Methodist is one who has 'the love of God shed abroad in [one's] heart.'"[1]

Methodism's story is a story of God's love. We receive that love through God's grace. God's grace is offered freely to all in Jesus Christ through the Holy Spirit. In the story of Methodism, grace is received and shared through practices of Christian faith and discipleship. God shares it with us and through us, earnestly and relentlessly, until not only individuals are transformed, but whole communities are transformed through God's grace. The Methodist movement embodied in The United Methodist Church demonstrates a remarkable heritage of ministry. By participating in God's unfolding work, Methodists continue to participate in transforming countless lives over almost three centuries.

Early Methodism was a renewal movement within the Church of England. The Wesleys did not intend to create a new church. Through a small group of young adults searching for purpose and relationship with God, an initially modest movement steadily grew. Today, United Methodism has over six million members in the United States with another more than six million members outside the United States for a total of over twelve million members, which continues to grow. This means, while church membership across denominations in the United States experiences steady decline, United Methodism demonstrates growth and vitality across the world.

Knowing Who We Are: Sent by God

How is it that Methodism grew and continues to grow in such remarkable ways? How is it that Methodism built dozens of hospitals in the wake of the Civil War when resources and collaboration were scarce and continues to support hundreds of health care institutions and community ministries? How is it that Methodism consistently established schools for children with little accessibility to education? How is it that Methodism, a simple renewal movement deploying lay preachers and visitors with little to no access to education, established colleges, universities, and theological seminaries, which today total well over one hundred institutions of higher education? How is it that Methodism made room for women when there was no room for women's voices or leadership in society or churches, and advocated against the enslavement of persons generations before these causes were broadly considered?

Through Methodism the Triune God changed, and changes, the lives of countless through receiving and sharing the grace of the Triune God, Father, Son, and Holy Spirit. This grace is not merely a vertical grace only focused on the inner spiritual well-being of individuals. The grace found and shared in Methodism is a scripturally grounded grace that reinvigorates the imagination of individuals and transforms communities to participate in God's work in the world.

Through reading Scripture carefully and canonically, meaning as a whole story, John Wesley laid the foundations to support a simple, practical, generative movement. Wesley read Scripture for each verse and for the magnificent story of God's salvation and grace extended to all. Through Wesley's writing, teaching, and preaching, a distinctive scriptural imagination developed holding together salvation of souls, bodies, and communities. This imagination fueled the simple practical responsiveness of the Methodist movement to the Holy Spirit. Through studying Scripture, consistent prayer, and practices of love of God and neighbor, Methodism followed the Holy Spirit to facilitate the spiritual renewal of persons and to build structures to respond to the deep needs of society.

In this way Methodism was and is *missional*, which from Scripture means sent by God in ministry to the world. In John 20:19-21 we read, "As the Father sends me, so I send you." As God sends Jesus Christ, Jesus Christ sends the disciples and subsequently the church with the Holy Spirit to all creation.

Today, one important way The United Methodist Church's grace-filled missional purpose is described is in its mission statement, which appears in paragraph 120 of *The Book of Discipline, 2016*:

> *The Mission*—The mission of the Church is to make disciples of Jesus Christ for the transformation of the world. Local churches and extension ministries of the Church provide the most significant arenas through which disciple-making occurs.

At times the expectations related to disciple-making, particularly addressed in Matthew 28, assume that the role of making disciples is left to *human* responsibility. At times local congregations attempt to fulfill this responsibility through logistics such as signage and parking, marketing strategies, and programming. While these are often helpful practical strategies, Matthew 28 and the whole of the Scripture text offer more.

A close look at Matthew 28, and particularly John Wesley's commentary on these verses, reveals the meaning of the verb "discipling," namely that *God is the primary actor in disciple-making*. This offers a richer and wider tapestry for seeing our role as baptized members of the body of Christ, and as members of The United Methodist Church, in God's work in the world. God, in Jesus Christ, through the Holy Spirit, inspires us to participate in God's work transforming individuals and communities.

The verb "to make disciples," when examined in the Greek—which John Wesley did in his *Explanatory Notes upon the New Testament*—reveals a collaborative relationship between God and those God calls to the practice of discipling and evangelism. The verb *matheteuein* or literally "to disciple" only occurs four times in the entire New Testament, three times in Matthew (13:52; 27:57; and 28:19) and once in Acts (14:21). This rare verb indicates the primary actor in discipling is not humanity, but *God*, into whose mission we are invited. Understanding our human role in discipling as invited participants changes our perspective on participation in God's work. With Matthew's imperative to "go and make disciples," Jesus Christ invites us to share God's love and grace with others, participating in God's transformation of all creation by inviting others to participate in it as well.

The purpose of this book is to offer those involved in church life a deeper understanding of the distinctives of Methodism to strengthen our sense of identity, better express our beliefs, and deepen our connections within The United Methodist Church. This study engages a set of important values and characteristics that make Wesleyan/Methodist Christianity distinctive—such as God's grace for all and sanctification as tangible transformation in individuals, communities, and creation.

Description of Chapters

The following describes each chapter of the study, which includes reflection upon major characteristics of The United Methodist Church as it grows from the early Wesleyan movement into its embodiment today. As we focus on our origin story and significant themes of our shared narrative, I hope we will see the threads of faithfulness and hope that guide us into the future. The chapters are organized in three sections: grace, connection, and beliefs.

In chapter 1, "Finding Grace," we recognize the distinctiveness of early Methodism as a movement of renewal, not of protest or disagreement based on doctrinal disputes. Methodism from its very beginning to the present continues to be a missional movement, one motivated by receiving and sharing God's grace. Alongside reflections on important aspects of our early narrative, chapter 1 also describes the defining doctrinal belief in Methodism, the role of God's grace. God's grace, as described in Scripture, includes several layers of God's love and forgiveness for and in us and all creation. In chapter 1 we reflect deeply on God's love for all in prevenient, justifying, and sanctifying grace.

Chapters 2, 3, and 4 describe significant characteristics of Methodism that continue to define our strengths and distinctiveness. Each of these three chapters describes a different yet overlapping component of Methodism as a renewal movement and eventually as a mainline Protestant denomination. From its beginnings, Methodism attentively nurtures individuals in personal relationships with the Triune God to receive God's grace in Jesus Christ through the Holy Spirit. At the same time, and quite distinct from other denominations, Methodism also participates in God's sanctification of communities by advocating for God's justice and compassion. Methodism's capacity to participate in God's grace offered to individuals and active in communities draws from careful study of Scripture and theological reflection.

Chapter 2, "Saving Small Groups," traces the significant role of small group participation throughout Methodism's story. In this chapter we explore distinctive contributions and dynamics within Methodist small groups that allow space for individuals to find, accept, and share God's grace with others. Methodist small groups, when practiced after the example of the earliest gatherings led by John Wesley, are distinctive among Christian traditions.

Chapter 3, "Local and Connectional," reflects on Methodism's distinctive connectional character. While local churches are the primary setting of our Christian experience and worship, Methodism is characterized by its connectionalism, which emphasizes mutuality and collaboration to participate in God's unfolding work in the world. Chapter 3 describes the local church, its role in disciple-making, worship (including composing and singing hymns), and connection to the broader denomination. When viewed as a whole, Methodism's connection is structured for service to share God's grace.

Chapter 4, "Tenacious Mission," highlights the continuing practices of missional outreach by Methodists since our beginnings. Formed in small groups of Christian nurture, John Wesley and the early Methodists regularly practiced love of neighbor in their communities by visiting persons in need, including incarcerated, impoverished, or widowed persons as well as vulnerable children. Early Methodists continued practicing love of neighbor through coordinating initiatives of greater impact through microfinance, health care, and education. Methodism in the United States and across the centuries carries on this legacy.

Chapter 5, "Texts That Shape Us," explains the primary role of Scripture in the lives of Christians, especially United Methodists. Beginning with John Wesley and the early Methodists, this chapter reflects on the uniqueness of Scripture as God's revelation both through the inspiration of the Holy Spirit of its authors as well as its readers. This chapter describes John Wesley's careful and thorough practices of study and interpretation including the many resources, such as commentaries and translations in the original languages. John Wesley also valued doctrinal materials to assist with the interpretation of Scripture. This chapter gives an overview of our United Methodist doctrinal materials.

Chapter 6, "Growing in Grace," reflects on the strengths and hope of United Methodism for the present and future in light of current complexities that confront all of us. United Methodist churches in the United States are confronted with astounding challenges including rapidly aging congregations as well as declining membership. Yet the nation endures what the US Surgeon General described in May 2023 as an epidemic of isolation with increasing numbers of loneliness impacting not only the mental but also physical health of millions. Following the COVID-19 global pandemic beginning in 2020, many more realize the numerous pandemics that continue to threaten all of us from racial, ethnic, and gender prejudice to systemic poverty and economic disparities. The digital age presents severe threats to privacy, security, and mental health, yet also unfathomable opportunities for connection across the globe. United Methodism, drawing on our distinctive strengths of individuals spiritually nurtured in God's grace, grounded in Scripture, connected through worship and service, is distinctively, if not uniquely, poised to embody God's grace and justice in the world.

Methodists
search for,
accept, grow in,
and share
God's grace
with *holy tenacity*.

Holy Tenacity: Methodism's Story

The story of Methodism begins with John and Charles Wesley, two young adults searching for God's grace, and persists today after almost three centuries across the world among over twelve million participants with exponentially more impacted by its ministries. Throughout our story, Methodists search for, accept, grow in, and share God's grace with *holy tenacity*. John Wesley described himself when he wrote in his journal in the spring of 1739 in response to George Whitefield's seemingly risky and audacious field-preaching:

> I was "so tenacious of every point relating to decency and order that I should have thought the saving of souls almost a sin if it had not been done in a church."[2]

John Wesley's remarks remind me of some present-day Christians. Have we become similarly preoccupied with decency and order over and against God's ministry of salvation? Rather than a tenacious maintenance of decency and order—where are we called to practice holy tenacity participating in God's unfolding work to receive and share God's grace with all? I hope you find inspiration for your own practices of holy tenacity to receive and share God's grace. In preparing this book, I was reminded of the sheer beauty and compassion of God's grace in and beyond Methodism.

Beginning in December 2021, I led a Bible study in my small, rural, local community, beyond any church buildings. This group of eight regular participants, along with frequent visitors, formed organically one evening at a coffee shop. The topic that drew us and kept us gathered was God and the many embodiments of church.

As United Methodism and other denominations struggle to slow, much less reverse, decline, this group of eight unrelated, diverse individuals eagerly search for Christian community. In a town saturated with Christianity, ironically, most in the Bible study and those we encounter feel excluded, ignored, and criticized despite their hunger for and interest in the gospel of Jesus Christ. These Bible study participants teach me almost daily about the holy tenacity of God's grace for me and all creation. The Bible study participants also remind me of the early Methodist renewal movement and the holy tenacity that United Methodism continues to demonstrate in its most faithful of moments.

"Holy tenacity" embodies the Triune God's redeeming love for all by reflecting the light and holiness of God's love in authentic Christian relationships that offer glimpses of the joy and justice of God's unfolding work. Jesus sets the ultimate example of holy tenacity particularly in his teaching that embodies Scripture's salvation narrative. For me, holy tenacity describes God's work in us courageously and persistently to respond to the Holy Spirit's compelling us to share God's amazing grace in Jesus Christ despite expectations of appropriate Christian, or "churchy," behavior.

When we reflect on knowing who we are as United Methodists, I hope these themes of love, grace, missional connection, and holy tenacity resonate not just with who we were, but who we are and continue to be.

Loving Well

Implicit in John Wesley's words about tenacity and ministry is a central question about how to love well. We are called by the Triune God, in both Old and New Testaments, to love all God's creation—those with and without power, especially children. We are called to love the unloved and the unlovable—even Judas.

It is difficult to study the Scripture (and participate in Christian community) without having a sense of the whole biblical canon and its purpose. Through stories, poetry, and parables we learn about God's grace-filled relationship with humanity and creation. The Bible is often mistakenly described as a rule book—or even a reference manual. The Bible, Scripture, is a story. It is the most dramatic saga with an amazing twist ending ever. Scripture is the narrative of God's salvation for all creation. This does not mean there are not difficulties, challenges, expectations, and unrealized hopes as we read divinely inspired human composition. Scripture is about God's unrelenting love.

The primary guideline for the Bible study gathering, agreed upon almost instantly, is "no judgment" among and beyond participants. The group's rationale is based on their ubiquitous experience of receiving judgment from Christians and church members. Interestingly, the Bible is very clear regarding God's role as the author of salvation (see, for example, Psalm 62:7). Therefore, only God may save—or judge. Inspired by these biblical themes the Bible study agreed by consensus, "Our main role is to love God and love each other well."

Bible Study and Christian Practice Need Each Other

Christian communities, no matter how small or large, practice holy tenacity when they embody God's love, receiving and sharing God's grace. This can include random acts of kindness: paying for someone's snack at the drive-through or giving a bottle of water to someone in need. These are pleasantly welcome gestures. However, the truly counter-cultural gritty Christianity of sharing God's grace that invites repentance and forgiveness changes the world.

As we remember who we are as Christians and United Methodists, we study Scripture to learn about God's forgiveness extended to all in Jesus Christ, we stretch our imagination and very being when we receive and participate in God's grace. We discover the depths of love's possibilities in hearing the confession of a long-held deep wound of betrayal and the request for forgiveness. In offering that forgiveness we release the burden of the wound-wielder and receive God's healing for the wounded—that is the gospel of Jesus Christ.

Reading Luke's Gospel and reflecting upon Mary's Magnificat in the context of Jesus Christ's nativity, we discover how practicing holy tenacity extends into a world turned upside down, or perhaps right side up, by God's grace. Reading the Magnificat together in the Bible study small group, we discovered how to lament the persistent oppression of systemic poverty and gender exploitation—even in rural Texas among quite different political affiliations. It is in our mutual laboring to listen and tenaciously love one another, even in that small group, that we find ourselves laboring together with the Holy Spirit to release victims and victimizers from the oppressive systems through mutual empowerment to participate in God's grace—and God's changing the world.

Bible study and Christian practice need each other—over and over again, a mutually reinforcing rhythm that moves us toward holiness. The early Methodists came to know this. Our formation as Christian disciples begins at baptism and continues throughout our lives as we participate in God's graceful work of sanctifying us in love.

When We Look Together, God Is Everywhere

The holy tenacity of this Bible study persists each week through God sightings. At the beginning of our gathering, each participant shares where they see God at work in their lives and community. No matter how sad, angry, guilty, or grumpy, we share about God's work of love in our lives and in the world. And, if I cannot see God, my neighbor describes God's work in and through me. The testimonies that unfold during these initial minutes set the tone for our prayers and biblical study. We've discovered that the more we practice seeing God, the more of God's grace and work in the world we see.

Whether in or beyond church buildings, God's Holy Spirit is moving in and among us, including United Methodists, inspiring holy tenacity. In reading this book and remembering who we are as Methodists in the Wesleyan tradition, I hope we will be encouraged in our faith and love of God and neighbor. As you read, let's reflect together: to what tenacious holiness is God calling us and our communities?

CHAPTER 1
FINDING GRACE

Knowing who we are begins with understanding our origin stories, or how the Methodist movement emerged. In this first chapter, we explore highlights of early Methodism's story, which is characterized by searching for and finding grace. The Methodist movement emerged as a renewal movement within the Church of England. Different from many other Christian traditions, Methodism did not form as a protest in reaction to conflict over beliefs. The main characteristic of the Methodist movement is its missional nature.

The early Methodist movement—above all else—was missional and evangelistic. While other denominational traditions often trace their roots to disagreements regarding confessional or theological points, the Wesleyan tradition emerged from a missional imperative. However, the contemporary language of mission and evangelism with which we are familiar was not in use during the eighteenth century. John Wesley summarized his understanding of Methodism's purpose: "What may we reasonably believe to be God's design in raising up the Preachers called Methodists? A. To reform the nation and, in particular, the Church; to spread scriptural holiness over the land."[1]

Our Methodist story, the setting, main characters, and plot frame our beliefs, which we share with other denominations among the many branches of the Christian family tree. Methodist beliefs distinctively rely on a robust understanding of grace grounded in Scripture. After exploring highlights from Methodism's origin story, we will explore a Methodist understanding of grace. Within Christianity, and Methodism specifically, the doctrine of grace is the central theme of God's relationship to humanity.

Where Are We From?

When meeting new people one of the earliest questions asked of one another is, Where are you from? Often this question even precedes introductions including the question, "What is your name?" Whether meeting neighbors, coworkers, friends, particularly those with whom we find ourselves journeying on buses, trains, and planes, this question helps to locate us on a larger landscape. At its best, this question expresses interest and care for another's identity.

At a gathering of work colleagues sitting around a table sharing a meal, we inquired about the places from where our parents and relatives originate. Where are you from? Every response shared pieces of an intricate puzzle in an effort to assemble recognizable identities—and reveal plotlines to our stories. Some of us have relatives from the South, many farmers. Some relatives from the Mid-Atlantic settled before the Revolutionary War. Others described relatives in urban areas, gateway cities, populated by neighborhoods of immigrants, some arriving through Ellis Island generations ago. Still others arrived much more recently. Simply the mention of a nation or region can provide a picture depicting scenes in a longer story, some full of joy and possibility, others of painful loss from war, persecution for beliefs, or simply ethnicities.

Where are you from? Every response carries layers of nuanced narrative and chunks of puzzle pieces offering windows into our identities and stories. Stories of pain, but also of hope.

The story of Methodism is set in a distinctive time and place within the story of the Church of England and reveals important layers about our identity, purpose, and beliefs. Methodism is technically Protestant, namely not Roman Catholic, similar to the Church of England. Methodism initially emerged as a renewal movement within the Church of England.

The Church *in* England shifted to the Church *of* England as a result of the Reformation Parliament (1532–35) with the monarch, Henry VIII, as head of the church rather than the pope and the service conducted in English rather than Latin. Following the death of Henry VIII considerable turmoil ensued with monarchs taking conflicting sides in ongoing struggles between reestablishing Roman Catholicism and cultivating Protestantism. This turmoil cost many lives and caused destabilizing unrest across the nation contributing to England's vulnerability. During her reign, Elizabeth I brought relative stability through a "via media" or middle way incorporating aspects of the opposing Christian traditions within the Church of England. The Act of Uniformity (1559) negotiated a careful and nuanced set of standards for liturgy and doctrine, including adherence to doctrines demonstrated in the Book of Homilies and Book of Common Prayer.

The story of the Church of England is the backdrop upon which the story of Methodism emerges, including the parents of John and Charles Wesley. Samuel and Susanna Wesley significantly influenced their children. While Samuel, a graduate of Exeter College, Oxford University, was ordained in the Church of England, both Susanna and Samuel had nonconformist backgrounds. There were other Christian traditions outside the Church of England (including Roman Catholic, Baptist, and Unitarian) represented within England during this time called nonconformists, or dissenters. Adherents to nonconformist traditions were marginalized within society. While nonconformists—those not conforming to the Church of England—could gather with appropriate registration of their meeting houses, they could not vote, hold office, or participate fully in society. While John and Charles Wesley remained ordained within the Church of England throughout their lives, Susanna was buried in a nonconformist cemetery called Bunhill Fields along with Paul Bunyan and other well-known dissenters, across from Wesley's Chapel in London.

Susanna and Samuel raised their family while serving the parish of Epworth. Samuel, a published author who wrote a commentary on Job, enjoyed travel and time away from home where he occasionally incurred debts resulting in a brief incarceration. Susanna educated each of her children, including teaching the girls to read, even before they could sew, a highly unusual practice. She maintained close relationships through correspondence, including those with John and Charles into their adulthoods. In Samuel's absence, at the request of parishioners Susanna would host gatherings in their kitchen to pray and read Scripture. While careful not to preach or defy restrictions on women's ecclesiastic roles, Susanna clearly demonstrated pastoral gifts as well as theological wisdom. Through their correspondence Susanna informed John's theological contributions and leadership of the Methodist renewal movement.

A renewal movement within the Church of England, Methodism, and its identity and beliefs, does not appear out of nothing or *ex nihilo* but grows as a response to a particular narrative and set of circumstances. The Church of England, rooted in the larger contours of Christian tradition, expresses deep affinity for sometimes conflicting, but also complementary, Christian beliefs and practices. This prequel, or narrative from the Church of England, accounts for Methodism's wide yet deep roots and affinity for liturgical as well as revival worship styles.

Methodism Is Missional

Reflecting on who we are and from where we come as Methodists reveals important layers to our identities and narrative as a Christian community. Origin stories say a lot about an individual, congregation, or denomination. Among Christian denominations, Methodism is arguably unique.

The origin story of Methodism demonstrates one of our most significant characteristics: we are missional. We are unique because of our *missional* character.

What does "missional" mean? The word *mission* derives from the Latin root *missio* meaning sent or sending. When we think of mission, particularly within Christian communities, we think of missionaries or outreach work. This represents one aspect of the term's meaning. *Missio* also refers to the church. For example, in John 20:19-23 Jesus tells the disciples, "As the Father has sent me, so I send you." This use of "send" is also translated from the term *missio*, meaning sent by the Triune God in ministry to all the world. Like the disciples in the Gospel of John, Christians are sent, some literally, others metaphorically, in ministry.

For Methodists, not only do we share in God's mission as disciples sent in ministry to the world, but our origin story emerges from a missional imperative to share God's love with others.

Most Christian traditions, and current denominations, trace their origin stories to deep conflicts and significant differences in beliefs, doctrines, and interpretations of Scripture. Indeed, for some Christian traditions, particularly those taking shape in the last several hundred years—Baptists, Lutherans, and Presbyterians, to name some—the differences that resulted in the creation of Christian traditions were framed in violence and loss of life whether in battle, or through persecution and martyrdom. Thankfully, that is not Methodism's story.

Methodism's Story: Finding Grace

Admittedly, tracing a clear thread of historical origins for Methodism—a movement that developed spontaneously and was informed by multiple individuals, groups, and ideas—is complicated at best.

In 1781, John Wesley describes his perspective on the origins of Methodism in a pamphlet titled "A Short History of the People Called Methodists."[2] To describe its beginnings, John offers a narrative of the Three Rises of Methodism. This is a story of John and Charles, two young adults searching for and finding God's grace.

The story of Methodism, according to John Wesley, emerges in Oxford, England, among college students and young teachers. Charles Wesley, a student at Christ Church College invites his brother, at the time a new Fellow of Lincoln College, to meet with a small group. Some in the group were affluent with relative means like John and Charles; others from less resourced families such as William Morgan. These young adults, as young adults often do, noticed the contrast between what their elders and teachers declared and how these same accomplished and supposedly faithful Christians lived. Universities during this time, the 1720s, were religious institutions connected to the Church of England. However, the intentionality of practicing Christian faith in this time and context could be described as less than enthusiastic. One writer of the time described Oxford and its university as "comfortably slack." In response to this "slackness," the young Christian scholars gathered regularly to read the Greek New Testament, pray for one another, and hold one another accountable.

This gathering would multiply into several small groups, including one led by the well-known preacher and Methodist leader George Whitefield. During this "first rise" of Methodism, dated to 1729, participants pursued Christian practices to live into their salvation. Inspired by writers of earlier generations on spiritual disciplines and care of time, they kept detailed diaries. "The Holy Club" of early "Methodists,"as they were derisively called by detractors, used a cipher or code in their small journals that could fit into their coat pockets. The code allowed them to describe their activities throughout the day, sometimes every fifteen minutes, in a discreet way. Christian activities included reading Scripture, praying, fasting, attending public worship, as well as visiting and caring for incarcerated, impoverished, and vulnerable persons. In addition to tracking their practices throughout their days and weeks, they would evaluate their attitudes and responses to their Christian living using a list of questions. During the regular gatherings, participants would share their journals with one another seeking accountability, guidance, and encouragement.

John Wesley describes a "second rise" of Methodism marked by the Wesley brothers embarking to Georgia in 1735 as missionaries with the Church of England. This short season provided significant pastoral experience as they cared for established parishes among the settlers. John hoped to share the gospel with indigenous persons. In 1734, John had met a Creek chief, or "mico," named Tomochici during a tour of England, which most likely influenced John's intent. He looked forward to observing persons' initial encounters with the message of salvation to gain insight into effective Christian ministry. While he did interact with indigenous persons and shared the gospel, John was disappointed since those he met had already encountered the gospel among previous visitors, and often in negative ways.

During their time in Georgia, the Wesleys introduced one of the first hymnbooks to America, publishing a collection of psalms and hymns in 1737. The collection did not include contributions from Charles, since his poetic gifts had not yet fully emerged. The pastoral leadership provided by the Wesleys facilitated strong attendance at worship services and participation in small group formation. Unfortunately, John's zeal, and perhaps unhelpful reaction to unrequited affection related to Sophy

I felt my heart strangely warmed. I felt I did trust in Christ, Christ alone for salvation, and an assurance was given me that he had taken away *my* sins, even *mine* and saved *me* from the law of sin and death.

Hopkey, provoked critique as well as charges from community leaders. John abruptly departed Georgia late on a December night in 1737.

The "third rise" of Methodism, as described by Wesley, occurs in London following John's return from Georgia. John continues to search for spiritual and doctrinal assurance of salvation. The Moravian Peter Bohler would mentor John in spiritual and organizational matters. From Bohler, an ordained pastor and Moravian, John received the guidance, "Preach faith *till* you have it, and then, because you have it, you *will* preach faith." For Bohler, there are no degrees of faith, only salvation by faith alone accompanied by fruits. Following his brother Charles three days prior, John experienced assurance (a fruit of justifying grace) on May 24, 1738, when his heart was "strangely warmed." The significant experience occurred when after evening prayers in London's St. Paul's Cathedral, he attended a society meeting nearby on Aldersgate Street. Another participant read Luther's Preface to Romans, which John describes in his journal:

> About a quarter before nine, while he was describing the change which God works in the heart through faith in Christ, I felt my heart strangely warmed. I felt I did trust in Christ, Christ alone for salvation, and an assurance was given me that he had taken away *my* sins, even *mine* and saved *me* from the law of sin and death.[3]

John's assurance accompanied his development as an organizational leader in London and Bristol where he contributed to the organization of small groups and developed outreach efforts within the early Methodist renewal movement.

John and Charles Wesley never left the Church of England. However, John finally, after decades of intense discernment in the midst of pressures from all sides, participated in rogue ordinations in 1784, late in his life and ministry. While an act contrary to the practices of the Church of England, those ordained—Thomas Coke, Richard Whatcoat, and

Thomas Vasey—immediately departed for pastoral work in the nascent United States. During the Revolutionary War, most if not all Church of England priests had returned home, leaving many without pastoral leadership and access to the sacraments. So, this "rogue" act on the part of John Wesley served a missional purpose and did not result in his expulsion from the priesthood of the Church of England. When John Wesley died, he remained an ordained priest within the Church of England. Indeed, the ordinations of John and Charles Wesley are memorialized in Oxford Cathedral with a marker near the spot where the ordinations occurred.

In subsequent chapters we will follow threads from early Methodism through later scenes of our narrative to acknowledge contributions and explore characteristics of our current United Methodism. Significant threads from our origin story include an earnest search for God's grace, accepting God's grace, taking risks to learn more about and organize to share God's grace in mission.

In the next section, we unpack defining themes of Methodist doctrine, which finds its deep roots in scriptural understandings of grace. Drawing from Scripture, grace includes nuanced layers or kinds of grace. The following describes layers within a Methodist understanding of grace informed by John Wesley's sermon and a group of friends who asked me to lead a Bible study.

From Grace to Good Works: What Is Salvation?

Accepting and relying on God's grace for salvation is the most important component of Christian faith. Often, we neglect to attend to the most pressing truth about God's grace and salvation: there is nothing more, or anything less, one can do to earn God's love and eternal salvation. Nothing. One needs only to accept God's love and grace. Acceptance, that is all.

Yet as a pastor and teacher of pastors, I experience considerable misunderstanding and even concern among Christian believers about God's grace and salvation. Lifelong experienced Christians as well as those new or outside the church have profound questions: What is salvation? Who is saved? Are good works required for salvation? These are similar questions to those of the early Methodist renewal movement.

Recently I was invited to teach a Bible study, as I mentioned in the introduction, among people feeling actively excluded from church. Each week someone grieved their inability to "do better" and their concern for not deserving God's love. Every week. This, even though each week we talked about God's unconditional love and grace in Jesus Christ and how our desire to participate in Christian practices is a grateful response to God's unwavering grace. I identify with this deep concern. John Wesley and the early Methodists did too.

While biblical texts clearly describe salvation by grace alone, a theme emphasized among Protestants, confusion remains about the place of good works. Though we affirm we are saved by grace alone, we find good works to be a tempting functional alternative means of gaining God's— and perhaps others'—favor.

Salvation Now . . . and Not Yet

First, let's reflect on the meaning of salvation through a Wesleyan frame. While salvation from God in Jesus Christ through the Holy Spirit does include afterlife, resurrection of the body, and reuniting with the communion of saints, those dimensions only scratch the surface of a scriptural understanding of salvation. The term "salvation" in Scripture is translated from the Greek term *sozo,* which envisions wholeness.

When surveying Scripture to better understand the meaning of God's salvation in our lives, we find many more layers than simply an eternal rest in heaven. In every reference, salvation is God's work, God's work alone. According to biblical scholars, salvation in the Old and New Testaments is both individual and social—as well as cosmic, since Scripture tells us all creation will be redeemed. Salvation also includes as many as six dimensions: economic, social, political, physical, psychological, and spiritual—and can be emphasized in this order (see David Bosch on Luke). John Wesley and the early Methodists shared these scriptural themes relating to salvation.

John Wesley provides context for understanding salvation in the opening paragraph of his sermon "The Scripture Way of Salvation" written in 1765, which represents his most mature theology. John explicitly states salvation is not only "going to heaven or paradise." According to John, "The end is, in one word, salvation: the means to attain it, faith." He continues "It is easily discerned, that these two little words, I mean faith and salvation, include the substance of all the Bible, the marrow, as it were, of the whole Scripture."

John Wesley describes salvation as available now. Living into the wholeness of God's salvation in Jesus Christ through the Holy Spirit for us through grace alone changes everything. When we receive God's grace, we experience salvation, not only the ultimate wholeness of union with the Triune God, but the assurance now of reconciled relationships with God and others. Through our baptism we are initiated into the body of Christ and commissioned to love God and neighbor in our words and lives. This new identity as children of God gives us purpose and peace in the midst of a troubled world as we participate in God's unfolding work.

What Is Grace?

"For by grace you have been saved through faith, and this is not your own doing; it is the gift of God—not the result of works, so that no one may boast."

(Ephesians 2:8-9)

God offers grace to all. Grace is the free gift of God's redeeming love in Jesus Christ through the Holy Spirit. In *The Book of Discipline of The United Methodist Church, 2016,* a description of grace precedes the discussion of "Distinctive Wesleyan Emphases" (para. 102). "By Grace we mean the undeserved, unmerited, and loving action of God in human existence through the ever-present Holy Spirit." *The Book of Discipline* continues, "The restoration of God's image in our lives requires divine grace to renew our fallen nature." According to United Methodist resources, Grace pervades all of creation and is universally present. Grace is God's presence to create, heal, forgive, reconcile, and transform human hearts and creation.[4]

John Wesley provides further guidance for understanding grace in his sermon "The Scripture Way of Salvation," in which he categorizes grace as prevenient, justifying, and sanctifying.

Prevenient Grace

As I mentioned earlier, I led a Bible study in my small, Texas, rural community beyond any church buildings. This group of eight regular participants, along with frequent visitors, formed organically one evening at a coffee shop. Well, initially some gathered at a bar, but we transitioned to a local coffee shop. However, folks felt more comfortable at the bar. Eventually we would meet next to a funeral home.

It began when I was visiting a neighbor. She had been unable to find a church home where she felt comfortable and wondered openly to me about God questions. As she noticed others listening from surrounding tables, she invited them to join us. While I did not know anyone beyond my neighbor, since I am an outsider to this small, rural community, everyone else knew everyone, their relatives, and their stories, *all* their stories. The Holy Spirit gathered a group of people who were wounded by the church and its members, but who were also persistently searching for God. On the surface it appeared a shared interest in God drew us together. That is true, but there is more.

God's prevenient grace drew us together. It was God's prevenient grace in Jesus Christ through the Holy Spirit within each of us, created in the image of God, yearning for the restoration of that image that drew us and kept us gathered. God's prevenient grace precedes our awareness, leading us toward God and one another for the purpose of receiving God's grace and salvation. Prevenient grace means the grace that "comes before."

Can you imagine for a moment? Every person is created in the image and likeness of God, though fallen. And God's grace beginning with prevenient grace is consistently working within each of us. Prevenient grace precedes, or comes before, one's awareness of God pushing and pulling us toward God and Christian community. Prevenient grace is consistently guiding persons created in the image of God to seek God's grace and salvation. Yet so many feel unwelcome, actively excluded, or at best uncomfortable among practicing Christians. Let that sit for a moment.

When talking about grace, particularly when drawing from Scripture, we often begin with our own experience and need for grace. We all carry original sin resulting from our existence post the Fall of Adam and Eve. As Scripture teaches, specifically Romans 3:23, "Since all have sinned and fall short of the glory of God." Creation needs grace because of the pervasiveness of sin introduced to creation at the Fall. United Methodists believe the biblical truth that all creation is created good, and humanity is created in God's image. Yet because of the Fall, all are born into original sin, the corruption and inclination toward separation from God including evil. For John Wesley, sin includes anger, self-will, and pride.

Prevenient grace for Methodists leads to our awareness of sin and discernment of conscience, knowledge of right and wrong, and ultimately repentance. This starting place focuses on our human experience, which is not wrong. However, our experience is not actually the starting place. The starting place for all creation is God. Let's begin instead with God's activity. When we enlarge the frame and begin at the beginning, we see God's work of creation—heaven, earth, and including all humanity—is declared good. God declared all creation, yes all, good.

Throughout the creation narrative beginning in Genesis 1:1 God consistently declares creation good. "God saw that the light was good" (Genesis 1:4). God saw that the earth and sea, vegetation, sun and moon, creatures in the sea, air, and on land were all good (Genesis 1:10, 18, 21, 25). Then God said, "Let us make humans in our image" (Genesis 1:26). "God saw everything that he had made, and indeed, it was very good" (Genesis 1:31). One essential purpose of grace, initiated by prevenient grace, is to restore the image of God, God's goodness, in persons.

Who Can Be Saved?

As you can imagine, Christians represent many different perspectives on interpreting Scripture. In John Wesley's understanding of grace, specifically prevenient grace, he chooses to advocate for one of these perspectives relating to who may be saved. For John Wesley, most (if not all) Methodists and many others called Arminians (or followers of Jacob Arminius, 1560–1609), anyone *can* be saved. This is described by the Arminian concept of *universal atonement.*

Universal atonement describes God's offer of salvation in Jesus Christ through the Holy Spirit to all. Universal atonement is not the same as universal salvation, the belief that all will be saved. Universal atonement does not guarantee universal salvation. Universal atonement draws from Scripture the truth that God desires to redeem all creation through Jesus Christ in the Holy Spirit. So all *may* be saved, but not all *will* be saved. Like with Adam and Eve, God gives us choice, or free will.

God forgives all.
God's grace is
given to all.

While there is nothing we can do, or not do, to earn God's salvation, God gives us the choice to accept, or not, a relationship with God and salvation by grace alone.

Embodying the notion of universal atonement in the small, rural, community Bible study was one of the most freeing and wonderful and at the same time one of the most challenging of practices. For those finding acceptance, affirmation, and accountability, some for the first time, it was a wonderful community like no other they had experienced. And yet for some of the same folk, practicing that acceptance, expressing affirmation, and practicing loving accountability with others—actual others, with many shared histories and hurts—was excruciating. We consistently reminded ourselves, both when we needed to receive and give love, the Triune God loves and forgives—me—and "them." God forgives all. God's grace is given to all.

Interestingly, around 1787, late in John Wesley's life and ministry, John Wesley was especially proud that the Methodists were distinguished by their willingness to admit *anyone* as society members who had the searching faith of a servant. Yes, anyone. This is prevenient grace. Just like I learned in Sunday school, God's Riches At Christ's Expense—GRACE—for all.

Are Only Humans Saved?
All Creation Will Be Restored

Drawing on Scripture, Wesley makes an important assertion about the restoration of all creation. In addition to humanity's access to grace to restore the image of God in persons, animals also receive redemption. In his sermon "The General Deliverance," John Wesley argues that all creation is influenced by the Fall of humanity described in the biblical narrative of Adam and Eve. While animals are not created in the image of God, all creation enjoyed living in relationship with God and one another. As a result of the Fall, all creation is impacted, including the introduction of illness and suffering to animals. John Wesley turns to Isaiah 11:6-9:

> *The wolf shall live with the lamb; the leopard shall lie down with the kid; the calf and the lion will feed together, and a little child shall lead them. The cow and the bear shall graze; their young shall lie down together; and the lion shall eat straw like the ox. The nursing child shall play over the hole of the asp, and the weaned child shall put its hand on the adder's den. They will not hurt or destroy on all my holy mountain, for the earth will be full of the knowledge of the LORD as the waters cover the sea.*

Through the Triune God's grace, all creation is ultimately restored into reconciled and full harmony.

Justifying Grace

Like John Wesley, Methodists can struggle actually to accept God's offer of salvation through grace alone. Admittedly, John searched tirelessly, diligently, intensely—for a decade, if not more—not just for an understanding of God's grace, but for an experience of assurance that he was saved.

Beginning as a student and then young scholar at Oxford in the 1720s John could see the delusion at best and hypocrisy at worst among his classmates and colleagues. When Charles invited John to lead a small group of similarly minded young adults, it did not resolve John's search for grace, but gave him a community. John even convinced Charles and others to travel to Georgia on a winter crossing, putting their very lives at risk to serve as missionaries in Georgia, also in search of assurance. John was mesmerized by the Moravians' peace and calm demonstrated as they recited psalms during a deadly storm on their sea journey. He yearned for the same and finally found, at least for a time, assurance of his salvation at the society meeting on Aldersgate Street in London.

Justifying grace, or justification, is the work of God in persons imputing Jesus Christ's righteousness by planting the seeds of salvation, pardoning or forgiving sin through faith. Justification is the gift of grace through faith alone and is the work of God in Christ through Jesus's atonement, life, death, and resurrection. Justification is what God does for us in Christ. Justification results in a new relationship between God and the believer. Through justification we are freed from the guilt of sin and receive assurance of our salvation. Assurance is the witness of God's Holy Spirit with our spirit that we are children of God. This is not necessarily an assurance of heaven or final salvation, but an assurance of God's love for us as children of God.

Baptismal practices from the early church demonstrate God's work in justification, through the symbolism of white robes in which the new converts were wrapped as they ascended from immersion in the baptismal font. One of my greatest gifts of participating in God's ministry is wrapping beloved children of God in white towels as they emerge from their baptismal waters having died to sin and claiming life in Christ. They are now clothed by God in Christ's righteousness through justifying grace working in them.

However, for Methodists and Arminians, because backsliding is possible, justification does not indicate "once saved always saved." It is possible, just like in any relationship, to refuse God's grace after receiving justification. And because of God's infinite and unconditional love, the offer of salvation by grace alone can be received again and again and again. While backsliding is possible, as is the occasional need to rededicate one's relationship with the Triune God, United Methodists do not re-baptize. Baptism, a sacrament, or an outward and visible sign of an inward and spiritual grace, indicates God's activity, which does not fail.

In Sunday school I learned about God's justifying grace "just as if I never sinned." In response to justifying grace, one repents of sin and receives an assurance of one's salvation. For United Methodists drawing on Scripture and John Wesley, justification most often occurs as an event, not a process. At justification the process of sanctification begins.

Sanctifying Grace

Sanctification is God's work through the Holy Spirit in us. John Wesley describes sanctification as "saved from sin, and perfected in love." Through sanctifying grace God's image is renewed in us as we grow in holiness, evidenced in our expressions of love for God, neighbor, and creation. In sanctification Christ's righteousness is imparted to us. Sanctification is a real change in the life of believers. Through sanctification one is freed from the power of sin, although backsliding is still possible—and probable. Sanctification is most often a process that begins in persons at the time of justification. In sanctification one lives into the changed relationship with God and is changed from within by God's Holy Spirit. Because of sanctifying grace we find ourselves participating in good works and growing into an ever-deepening faith, not to earn grace but as its resulting fruit that nurtures further growth—or as Wesley described it, "perfected in love."

Good Works: Growing in Holiness

A Christian's good works follow one's justification and demonstrate a grateful response to God's love and grace in Jesus Christ. John Wesley even goes as far as to name good works as means of grace because in doing good works, we are nurturing God's sanctifying work, holiness, in us.

John Wesley offers a helpful perspective on the role of good works. Wesley struggled for much of his early life and ministry with the role and place of good works in salvation. To make his point, Wesley argues there are no good works until after justification, at salvation's beginning. For Wesley, any good works prior to one's acceptance of God's justifying grace can only function as a futile attempt to earn God's grace as explained in his sermon "Justification by Faith."

When Christian believers practice good works, we respond to God's love in gratitude by accepting the biblical invitation to love God and neighbor. Good works respond to God's gift of grace, and through those good works, God brings us to share in God's holiness and justice. As Wesley explained in "Justification by Faith," good works follow justification.

> No works done before justification are done as God hath willed and commanded them to be done...if we only consider, God hath willed and commanded that "all our works" should "be done in charity;"...in love, in that love to God which produces love to all [hu]mankind. But none of our works can be done in this love, while the love of the Father (of God as our Father) is not in us."

Sanctification, according to Wesley in this sermon, "is the immediate fruit of justification." Through sanctifying grace in us, believers grow in holiness.

Through good works a very careful and nuanced process occurs during sanctification to facilitate the growth of holiness in us. Scripture employs agrarian metaphors to demonstrate God's work of holiness through the practices of cultivation when growing a garden. While the farmer prepares the soil, plants the seeds, irrigates, weeds, and harvests, God alone produces the fruit.

A related metaphor offers contrast. The objective is not simply any growth, but rather fruit, the fruits of holiness. A tremendous amount of growth occurs in a swamp. However, a swamp seldom produces fruit. Therefore, good works or means of grace focus God's work in us, renewing the image of God, and growth in holiness.

Holiness is the reflection of God's image and love in our lives. Holiness through God's sanctifying grace provides what John Wesley describes as "salvation now." This occurs through our participation in good works but is not a direct result of good works. Holiness is God's work in us. We do not seek to earn God's grace anxiously worrying about our worthiness. Accepting God's grace in Jesus Christ and receiving the Holy Spirit opens us to following the example of Jesus and growing in holiness.

Following the mass shooting in Uvalde, Texas, on May 24, 2022, at Robb Elementary School, where nineteen students and two teachers were killed in addition to many more injured, one of the Bible study participants felt called to organize a gathering for prayer. She did not belong to a church, and if we are candid, did not feel comfortable in a church building. With help and encouragement, she organized and led a prayer vigil as well as a fundraiser in my neighbor's bar for the families of the Uvalde shooting victims. Several of the Bible study folks participated in the leadership of the vigil. I composed an order of worship with Scripture texts and prayers.

We were not sure how the "regulars" would receive the prayer vigil. This was not a church crowd. The venue is a small one. We hoped for eight to ten folks to allow us to pray publicly if not with them, then near them. We began, some nervously, at 6:30 p.m. By 6:40 p.m. the place, which, remember, is not large, was full. Over thirty folks quietly appeared. The television monitors remained on, but all the sound was muted. We recited the Twenty-Third Psalm together. We concluded with the Lord's Prayer, together again. And we passed the peace. No one fussed, mumbled, or coughed. Just peace, quiet, and oneness in grief, petition, and support. The bar, a rural Texas town's corner sports bar that served beer, was transformed into a space where heaven and earth seemed close.

An unlikely, yet respectful and solemn crowd gathered at the bar grateful for space to share their pain and "do" something. The fundraiser resulted in thousands of dollars raised that evening for a grieving family known by many. Within a week $10,000 was raised—all in cash. These are not rich or even middle-class folks. Many people farm, work shifts in factories, contribute to service occupations. The evidence of sanctifying grace working in and through persons was stunning. We saw fruits of God's holiness through the love demonstrated in prayers, worship, consolation, and in overwhelming generosity.

In the Bible study, though there is still struggle and doubt, each participant has come to accept God's grace and reflect God's image and love as we grow in holiness. For us, the group text is often a means of grace. There are spontaneous messages of love and prayers, particularly in celebrating God's amazing timing. There is organizing to provide meals, shelter, transportation, and celebration of children's birthdays in the midst of serious illness, grief, and transitions. In these messages and good works, I see God's renewed image reflected among each one—and the beauty is breathtaking.

Good works follow one's acceptance of God's grace in Jesus Christ through the Holy Spirit. Before this our works are not "good," or rather "God's works," though they may be well intentioned. Good/God's works facilitate the growth of holiness in believers. Through good works God's holiness produces fruit in our lives, that witness to others of God's love for all.

Entire and Final Sanctification

While there is not clear consensus on the concepts of entire sanctification and Christian perfection, these are important aspects of a Methodist identity and heritage. Indeed, John Wesley spent much of his time and energy explaining what entire sanctification, including Christian perfection, was *not*. According to John Wesley, entire sanctification and Christian perfection, which are synonymous, indicate perfect love and purity of heart. This is not absolute perfection as a state of being, but rather a continuous growth toward perfection, since the attainment of perfection is impossible in this life. John Fletcher, a close friend and colleague of John Wesley's, used the language of "second blessing" for entire sanctification.

The *via salutis*, or way of salvation, culminates for John Wesley and Methodists with final salvation, the end of one's earthly life and reunion with God. The focus of Wesley's understanding of salvation is its present tense as demonstrated in his last words in 1791, "The best of all is, God is with us." Every Methodist seeks to live a life of love, holiness of heart and life, and to spend eternity with the God of love.

Conclusion

The origin story of Methodism and its movement to renew the Church of England reminds us from where we come and who we are as a missional movement. Methodism did not emerge because of differences in beliefs, but rather out of dedicated commitment to share the gospel of Jesus Christ with all. A robust understanding of grace grounded in Scripture frames Methodist beliefs and practices. Our beliefs not only shape individual practices but facilitate the organization and deployment of mission and service. In the following chapter, we reflect on the significant roles of small groups in the early Methodist movement and their continued contribution today.

CHAPTER 2
SAVING SMALL GROUPS

At its heart, the "method" of Methodism is a way of bringing us together to know God more deeply by practicing our faith alongside others. In this chapter we will look at pieces from Methodism's story to see how we have shared that way of life through Christian formation. From our earliest days, small groups continue to be our best vehicle for people accepting God's grace in Jesus Christ and continuing their growth through the Holy Spirit. By practicing the means of grace in small groups and in daily individual life, we sustain and deepen Christian faith. We will also briefly explore the connection between small groups, preaching, and organization for mission. While this chapter features small group discipleship, chapter 3 focuses on the local church, the primary setting for preaching, and chapter 4 focuses on the Methodist's distinctive heritage of missional contributions. These three chapters describe components of a Methodist ecology for receiving and sharing God's grace.

Saving Small Groups

Small groups continue to be one of the most vital spaces for Christian formation with God and one another. There is an opportunity to study, reflect, challenge, and discover. In small group settings we can experience vulnerability and accountability in the midst of encouragement and hospitality. Seemingly endless research demonstrates the effectiveness of small group spaces for learning, character formation, community building, and recovery from trauma as well as addictions. Small groups are most often sites of God's gift of salvation.

Several aspects of the Bible study I led, first mentioned in the introduction and chapter 1, were typical of other small group studies in local churches. Each week when we gathered, I would light a candle, and we would pray together. We would share around the table our God sightings from the week—where we see God working in small and grander ways in our lives and the lives of our neighbors. If one of us could not think of a God sighting, another would narrate how they see God working in and through that one's life and witness. We also shared snacks, some homemade, some not. Over our first year together we read through Luke and Acts. We learned about Christian beliefs, including salvation, forgiveness, sin, the Triune God, resurrection, baptism, and the Lord's Supper.

This Bible study was also *unlike* any small group study I have ever encountered or imagined. A number of our group had experienced significant trauma. Each person in the group had experienced much more of life than I—and a few at half my age—in very painful ways. Largely for this reason, participants covenanted from the very beginning "to practice no judgment—of ourselves or others," since according to Scripture, judgment is God's alone. This practice endures, and like the early Methodist small groups, means all are welcome, all the time.

Our conversations were usually extremely loud with people interrupting and talking over one another, but not in a rude or malicious way. When reading the Bible and learning about a God we long for, and who lovingly longs for us, deeply rooted feelings had to be expressed. The energy, passion, realizations, love as well as frustration at one another and the churches some had encountered was palpable. While we shared snacks, we also shared bottles of wine, and most of all we shared real questions, pain, fear, as well as hope. The kind of questions that are gritty and direct and come from a place of immense vulnerability. All at one point seemed to feel like outsiders for circumstances in their lives stemming from a complicated mixture of events beyond their control and choices made.

While reading through Luke after Easter, we talked about baptism. To my surprise God's justifying grace was actively at work in the months of conversation, study, and prayer we shared. In the middle of one of our loud and rather animated discussions, one of the participants who was often quiet, made a confession of faith in Jesus Christ and asked to be baptized, then another, and the rest asked to reaffirm their baptisms. The energy in the room was electric. It took me some time to realize what was happening. After confessing faith in Jesus Christ, one immediately asked, "Can I be baptized? Will you baptize me, Laceye?" "What? You want to be baptized? You want me to baptize you? Well, yes, yes, of course!" There were hugs and tears all around.

I am intentionally not offering details related to situations and identities. Those are their details and their stories to tell. They were not related or even close friends upon coming together. But let me say, their separate stories remind me of those Paul encounters in the Acts of the Apostles. They have experienced more of life than I ever will because of gender, economic, cultural, and ideological challenges. They made the most beautiful confessions of faith in direct response to the Easter message that I could possibly imagine. This is God's grace—the prevenient, justifying, and sanctifying kind.

A Different Kind of Small Group?

When John Wesley writes about his appreciation for Methodist societies, one of the characteristics for which he is most proud is how the Methodists were distinguished by their willingness to welcome anyone into the society meetings. Methodists are even described as "friends to all."

While church announcements often say "all are welcome," is that really the case? One of the many things I learned from the Bible study described in chapter 1 is local churches, our members and leaders, are not always aware of how we are perceived. I am still absorbing and gaining understanding about how I unintentionally create exclusionary boundaries with my assumptions and expectations. Sadly, members of local congregations and sometimes pastors, hopefully unintentionally, create boundaries of exclusion with our expectations related not just to appearance, but behavior as well as appropriate responses and embodiments of Christian faith.

Within early Methodism, the small groups provided the primary space for cultivating leadership and discerning mission. John Wesley crafted a highly structured organization with various roles and responsibilities to facilitate the movement all nurtured in small groups. The following describes aspects of small groups organized in a specific location, The Foundery, the first base for Christian worship and formation in London. My colleague Randy Maddox, William Kellon Quick Professor Emeritus of Wesleyan and Methodist Studies, compiled extensive data from the Foundery Band lists, 1742–46 created by John Wesley. These lists include over 2,700 names across dozens of small groups.

John Wesley organized several kinds of small groups. We will look at three in particular: trial, penitent, and select societies. Every participant began in a trial band. Remember the one requirement for initial participation was a desire for salvation. To continue participating,

Methodists were distinguished by their willingness to welcome anyone into the society meetings. Methodists are even described as "friends to all."

disciples encouraged one another to practice the General Rules: to do no harm, do good/avoid evil, and attend the ordinances of God, which we will discuss further. The penitent bands were spaces for Christian nurture particularly for those struggling with spiritual or physical challenges. Select societies gathered leaders within the movement, including leaders of small groups, for ongoing spiritual nurture and mentoring.

Typically, participants began in trial bands, moved to penitent bands, then some into select societies, while the majority transitioned into a general category of bands usually organized by affinity (single female, married males, etc.). Occasionally, a group leader participating in a select band would encounter difficulties, sometimes referred to as backsliding, and shift back to a penitent band. The ethos of these groups was distinctive. We could imagine those shifting between groups, particularly someone transitioning from a select society to a penitent band, experiencing embarrassment, even shame. Alternatively, those in select society could seem proud and ambitious. However, this does not seem to have been the case. Instead, those in penitent bands for the first time, or not, seem to have welcomed the care, accountability, and encouragement. How refreshing to receive hospitality and nurture in the face of difficulties, obstacles, challenges even when these may be self-imposed. Participants in select societies, in a parallel way, did not see their placement as a reward that was earned and deserved, but rather a privilege and opportunity to learn and participate in ministry with others.

While teaching United Methodist Studies over the last almost twenty-five years, I have wondered out loud with students, because of this authentically Christian culture among early Methodist small groups, about possible shifts and dynamics between these groups. Specifically, I wondered if there is any record of a small group leader, also a participant in a select society, who had subsequently spent time in a penitent band

and later returned to a select society. The implications of this possibility are whether a small group leader could return to leadership after experiencing significant difficulties indicated by time in a penitent band in the midst of or as a pause in their leadership roles.

The short answer is yes. A small group leader, participating in a select society, could spend time in a penitent band after taking on their leadership role and return to a role as a small group leader. After examining the over 2,700 names on the Foundery band lists between 1742–46, as many as seven names appear chronologically in lists for select, then penitent, followed by select participants. While statistically a very small sample, in the scheme of God's unfolding work in the lives of Christian disciples, nothing is insignificant. The small groups that contributed to the early Methodist renewal movement within the Church of England provided a fruitful and welcoming space for the nurture of Christian faith among believers.

The capacity for a community to allow participants, even a small number, to step out of leadership to receive care, accountability, and nurture in my experience is astounding. So many of our social interactions, particularly in the current context of social media and exaggerated news, are fraught with insecurity, shame, embarrassment, and facades of perfection. In the early small groups organized at the Foundery in London from 1742–46, approximately seven leaders slipped, whether because of their own choices or unforeseen and uncontrollable circumstances. They left the select society focused on leadership formation to return to the space of penitence. In that space they did not receive punishment or scorn, but rather compassion, nurture, and encouragement. Because of this hospitality and ongoing care, made possible by God's grace in and among the participants in each kind of small group, those seven souls returned to leadership roles. This is one of the distinctive gifts of Methodism.

Counting Conversion

While "growth" in early Methodism did not ignore numbers, it primarily emphasized individuals' and communities' growth in grace through relationship with God and neighbor. In the following pages, we will look at the expansion of early Methodism through field preaching and networks of societies, or small groups, that made up circuits of local faith communities.

The Methodist renewal movement began in 1739 in Bristol with George Whitefield's field preaching among the coal miners of Kingswood. Upon Whitefield's invitation, John Wesley arrived in Bristol in late March 1739 to take Whitefield's place among the societies or small groups there. On learning of Whitefield's preaching in the open air, John remarked that he could "scarce reconcile [himself] at first to this strange way of preaching in the fields."[1] While open-air preaching was not illegal, it was highly irregular, especially among respectable clergy in the Church of England. John wrote that at the time he was "so tenacious of every point relating to decency and order that [he] should have thought the saving souls almost a sin if it had not been done in a church."[2]

Jesus's Sermon on the Mount, John's text for April 1, provided a persuasive example alongside his seeing Whitefield preach to approximately 30,000 persons. The following afternoon John "submitted 'to be more vile'" and preached in the open air by his estimate to 3,000–4,000. During his first month in Bristol, John estimated a total attendance of 47,500 persons at his field preaching, an average of 3,000 per event. Charles was skeptical of the practice of field preaching, particularly the excessive numbers reported by Whitefield and John.[3]

Presumably, these field preachers felt some need to justify their irregular practice, leading to the emphasis upon such staggering numbers. His skepticism waned following his reluctant preaching at Moorfields on June 24, 1739, to a crowd he calculated at 10,000. The large crowd convinced him it was a work of God's will. John, Charles, and Whitefield continued to preach in the open air attracting tremendous crowds, Whitefield usually attracting the largest. Methodist preachers addressed crowds not just in fields, but in a variety of unusual settings that included prisons, gallows, graveyards, market squares, mines, and at times a convenient spot under a tree.

Wesley remained wary of placing too great an emphasis on field preaching. Even with the remarkable numbers that came from it, he focused on the leadership of the movement that would shape it into a foundation for growth in grace.[4] According to Heitzenrater, John suggested, "To avoid giving needless offense, we never preach *without* doors when we can with any conveniency preach *within*." The movement would expand gradually; it would "go a little and a little" from the society meetings "so a little leaven would spread with more effect and less noise, and help would always be at hand."[5] In leading the early Methodist renewal movement, John's goal was to "spread scriptural holiness" not to create a "wildfire" but rather to oversee and maintain a purposeful and sustainable rate of growth.

Although Whitefield and the Wesleys' preaching, particularly in the open air, is well documented for its impact, their preaching did not stand alone. Significant to understanding preaching as one aspect of the early Methodist renewal movement is the practice of preaching alongside the creation of societies, or small groups. Preaching in areas where religious societies such as bands and class meetings existed proved to be most effective.

In 1745 the Methodist Conference decided to try preaching wherever opportunities arose, without focusing on the formation of societies to nurture those responding. The results of the experiment were clear: preaching where small groups were formed, or were already in place, saw more people who sustained their faith over the long term. The Methodist small groups Wesley organized led to a greater number of people to be nurtured in faith. When these groups were not accessible, those moved by the preaching were often lost.

The experiment ceased in 1748, and the Conference turned its focus to the formation of societies. John noted in the Minutes: "Almost all the seed has fallen by the wayside; there is scarce any fruit of it remaining."[6] Although George Whitefield drew larger crowds and more attention, Wesley and his Methodist societies likely had a greater impact through the eighteenth-century revival preaching because of their emphasis on nurturing discipleship. According to Heitzenrater, quoting Wesley, "The preacher had little opportunity for instructions, the awakened souls could not 'watch over one another in love,' and the believers could not 'build up one another and bear one another's burdens.'"[7]

By 1750 the Methodist revival was a recognizable feature in Britain.[8] It was largely centered in London, and societies there numbered around two thousand, with approximately 10,000 members across England.[9] Nearly three dozen preachers in England, Wales, and Ireland were preaching on nine circuits, which served almost one hundred societies.[10] Into the 1760s, Methodism was quite different from twenty years earlier with over thirty circuits in England, Wales, Ireland, and Scotland. Nearly one hundred traveling preachers encouraged twenty thousand society members—still a relatively small number, the membership growing nationally by fewer than one thousand per year.[11]

By the 1770s, Methodism was also growing in America. In England, societies were steadily growing by approximately 1,600 members per year. However, about a quarter of the circuits showed a yearly decrease (and were marked with an asterisk in the Minutes), while some remained stable, and others grew. In 1775, Leeds was the second circuit to surpass 2,000 members, along with London, which was still at 2,500 after twenty years.[12]

In 1781, with continued steady growth there were 178 preachers, one for every 250 members, a constant ratio since 1767. The number of circuits had nearly doubled to sixty-three (in England), but only about a dozen had over 1,000 members. Interestingly, the asterisks in the Minutes formerly marking declining circuits now marked growing ones. Perhaps because more than twice as many circuits as in the worst previous year had lost members.[13] While growth was steady overall, this did not preclude the possibility for local decline or other setbacks.

In a 1748 letter to Vincent Perronet, a supporter and encourager of the movement, Wesley described the early Methodist renewal movement without placing great emphasis on numerical growth. The letter was later published as a pamphlet titled "A Plain Account of the People Called Methodists." In it, we find a focus on the key theological and practical themes that characterized the movement, namely, doctrine, organization, and mission growing from a shared commitment to "spreading scriptural holiness."[14]

Comfortably Slack

There are similarities between Wesley's eighteenth-century context and our contemporary context. Oxford University in the early eighteenth century reflected much of the situation within English society as a whole. One observer described Oxford as the "seat of good manners, as well as of learning," however "a comfortable slackness" prevailed in the spiritual and academic endeavors of the university, representing a low point in the history of the school.

Prior to and during John Wesley's lifetime (1703–91) a polemic developed between Anglo and Roman Catholics and Puritans (high church and low church). Wesley navigated this divide by emphasizing a "middle way." Wesley states that he was "early warned against laying, as the Papists do, too much stress…on outward works, or [as the radical Protestants do] on faith without works, which, as it does not include, so it will never lead to, true hope or charity."[15] According to Wesley the

Human beings are justified by faith alone in Jesus Christ and sanctified by the Holy Spirit that empowers human beings to engage in practices that shape a life of holiness.

balance between faith and good works, the following of virtuous tempers, and the use of all the means of grace that God provided would help one "have the mind that was in Christ and walk as he walked."[16]

Papist, a play on the term "papal" or "pope," was the designation used by Puritans to describe in a derogatory manner their perception of the Roman Catholic extreme emphasis upon outward works. *Antinomian*, literally against the law or without the law, was a derisive name used by the Roman and Anglo Catholics to describe the Puritans' emphasis upon faith without works or salvation by faith alone.

From Wesley's perspective, and Christian tradition generally, indeed one that takes into account the scripture canon as a whole, both of these emphases are essential to a faithful Christian witness. Human beings are justified by faith alone in Jesus Christ and sanctified by the Holy Spirit that empowers human beings to engage in practices that shape a life of holiness.

Similarities exist between Wesley's eighteenth-century English context and twenty-first-century North America. Some characterize religion in mainstream America as comfortably slack. Although Gallup demonstrates a pervasive spirituality across the American culture, in some polls up to 90 percent, this spirituality tends to run broad but shallow. Significant evidence exists that today's society in the United States is less religious (not necessarily Christian) than ever (47 percent), though some of the nonreligious describe themselves as spiritual (33 percent). This spirituality, although a broad/wide river flow, seems for the most part a shallow stream.

Twenty-first-century North America shows no evidence of recovery from the early twentieth-century fundamentalist/modernist controversy, a similar dynamic to that of the papists and antinomians of eighteenth-century England. Charles Darwin's book *On the Origin of the Species* was published in 1859, and you probably remember this book presented an argument for evolution. During this period a field of study emerged called biblical criticism, which included the examination of scripture's historicity and accuracy.

This movement developed into what some called Modernism (related to but not exclusively representative of Enlightenment "Modernism"). Modernism emphasized the historicity and therefore the humanity of Jesus, which encouraged social reform movements to alleviate the suffering of humanity. Emphasis upon social systems and legislative reform developed to the exclusion of individual spiritual formation. In response to this trend of humanism, including evolutionary theories, liberal theology, and biblical criticism, the five points of fundamentalism were composed from an 1895 gathering in Niagara—inerrancy of scripture, the divinity of Jesus Christ, the virgin birth, a substitutionary theory of the atonement, and the physical and bodily return of Christ. The term "fundamentalism" derived from a series of tracts titled *The Fundamentals* that were published between 1910 and 1915.

Although both fundamentalists and modernists emphasized scripturally grounded values, the division of these components and excessive emphasis resulted in several Protestant denominations—especially Baptist, Presbyterians, and Disciples of Christ—splitting into Fundamentalist and Modernist wings. Sadly, this dynamic has also caused division in Methodism with the formation of the Global Methodist Church as a split-off of The United Methodist Church. However, like Wesley, maintaining the via media or dialectical balance between these two extremes, without excluding either, seems an appropriate scriptural Christian witness and what United Methodism has worked toward. Thus, both the individual's faith in Jesus Christ with evidence of holy living that includes charitable expressions are both scripturally grounded and essential to faithful Christian discipleship.

For John Wesley spiritual nurture and accountability for his faith and others in small groups grounded the early Methodist renewal movement in response to the layered social dynamics framed by a "comfortable slackness." John and Charles recognized the sometimes quiet, but pervasive nature of this slackness among, in Wesley's early terminology, "almost Christians." From the Wesleys' perspective, it was not enough for Christian believers to claim faith in Jesus Christ. God's grace, while not needing dutiful response, once experienced individuals and communities of faith that felt powerfully drawn to respond. Faith in response to God's amazing grace resulted in individual and communal Christian practices to embody love of God and neighbor, which was encouraged and facilitated through small group nurture or "watching over one another in love."

"To Watch Over One Another in Love"

In his sermon, "Causes of the Inefficacies of Christianity," John Wesley laments that so many believers prefer spiritual techniques that promise immediate results—a struggle still too common in our own day. To resist and reform that desire for immediate transformation, the Wesleys oriented the early Methodist movement toward sustained connection in two key ways. Methodist Christians were not only connected to one another for mutual support and accountability but also to the overall movement's goal of forming believers in holiness of heart and life. In his sermon "Upon Our Lord's Sermons on the Mount, 4," John claimed that earnest Christian formation would not occur "without society, without living and conversing with [others]." *The early Methodist movement's distinctiveness was not in its innovation, but in a powerfully simple integration of doctrine and practice moving us toward a faithful embodiment of Christlikeness.*

In response to requests, John began holding regular gatherings for those wanting spiritual formation and nurture. He structured these gatherings in a way that resembled societies within the Church of

England at that time. Eventually they grew into networks of Methodist communities of faith, called circuits, across Britain. Sometimes referred to broadly as "united societies," these gatherings arising initially in Bristol included the basic form of the "class meetings" with a further breakdown into other, smaller and more particularly defined groups.

Class meetings usually consisted of ten to twelve members and were organized geographically. Along with participating in their class meeting as the essential vehicle of formation, Methodists would then, if inclined, also participate in a "band." Bands were smaller gatherings organized around an interest or demographic (for example, young married women, single men, and so on) and provided additional guidance and nurture beyond the class meetings.

These small groups, both classes and bands, provided opportunities for early Methodist laypersons, particularly women and young adults, to not only practice their faith and move into holiness of heart and life but they also became the best space for raising up leaders. Methodist laypersons in these groups would come to assume leadership roles such as leaders, lay assistants, stewards, and visitors of the sick.[17] In the early Methodist renewal movement, Methodist laypeople had greater influence than preachers or clergy in facilitating conviction, sanctification, and other significant spiritual experiences.[18] The most frequent social context for early Methodist conversions was solitude, followed by small groups, not larger preaching occasions.[19] Most individuals began participating in Methodist societies prior to their experience of justification. More than half received a spiritual experience (ranging from the subtle to the very dramatic) within the first year.[20]

The Methodist "way" is experiential first: we find ourselves in saving relationships in small group gatherings where we experience conviction and formation that precedes our experience of justifying grace. It's then, and in the continued context of these small groups, that we learn more about the doctrine of the church, encounter Scripture, and practice the means of grace. God's prevenience is revealed and embodied in saving small groups.

General Rules: Doctrine for Discipleship

In 1743, as the Methodist small groups continued to grow and a network among them expanded throughout England, John Wesley wrote a series of simple "rules" to give these groups a common form and way of life to share in together. The General Rules describe the gatherings as "a company of men [and women] having the form and seeking the power of godliness, united in order to pray together, receive words of exhortation, and to watch over one another in love, that they may help each other to work out their salvation."[21] While the one condition for admission remained—"a desire to flee from the wrath to come, and to be saved from their sins"—continuing to participate in one's small group meant showing evidence of fruitfulness found in following these three general rules: (1) by doing no harm and avoiding evil of every kind, (2) by doing good, and (3) by attending upon the ordinances of God.[22]

To this day, these General Rules stand like guideposts marking the course of Methodist life—they are part of our distinct understanding of doctrine. The General Rules and their description as means of grace show Christians within The United Methodist Church the way to practice their faith against the backdrop of our deep, historically shared doctrinal commitments. Individuals in covenant with their brothers and sisters in Christ nurture their faith in the Triune God together through common devotional practices like prayer and sharing in the Lord's Supper, while also serving their neighbors through practices of mercy. The first two rules relate, again, to the orientation of Christian life: they are about actions, what we do together, and how those actions are tangible, embodied expressions of mercy, grace, and love.

Christian practices
can be a deep river of
grace over and against
the shallow and
even dry streams of
modern spirituality—
and a comfortable
slackness.

The General Rules' third component, the "ordinances of God" consisted of what Wesley often referred to as the means of grace. In the context of their bands and classes, Christians would encourage one another in their Christian journeys by asking: How are you praying? Where are you serving others, visiting the sick and those who are imprisoned? By holding one another accountable to these practices, these believers helped one another come to know faith in the Triune God. Some of these means of grace emphasized individual spiritual growth through public and private prayer, Scripture study, confession, fasting, and participating in worship. Other practices were more about how one shared in God's mercy and love at work in the world, like feeding one's hungry neighbors; clothing those without adequate shelter; and visiting the imprisoned, sick, and afflicted. Interestingly, at times Wesley prioritized these works of mercy over individual devotional activities. He emphasized Methodists participating in acts of service as a way of correcting for a tendency he saw too often in the church in his day, where Anglican teaching and practice focused on personal devotion to the minimization or even exclusion of Christian service.

Means of Grace

These "ordinances" that John Wesley built into the pattern and shape of Methodist life go by many names: Christian practices, spiritual disciplines, and means of grace. No matter what you call them, Wesley did not intend for Methodists to see them as dull obligations or stale chores. These practices, and more important, being part of small groups where these practices were shared, encouraged, and engaged brought new and mature believers alike into freedom from self-interest and fear, to be replaced with peace and purpose, in relationship with God and neighbor. Christian practices can be a deep river of grace over and against the shallow and even dry streams of modern spirituality—and a comfortable slackness.

However, knowing the steps and mechanics of these practices does not automatically result in faithful participation and transformation. John Wesley referred to holy tempers. Holy tempers are like pathways or channels through our wills or inclinations. Faithful participation in the means of grace is like pouring water over stone so that over time the Holy Spirit wears new channels of holiness. An openness to God's work of holiness in us is far more crucial than the mechanics. The disciplines are not an exercise in willpower. Inner discipline, spirituality, and righteousness are rather a gift from God—sanctification—the work of God done in us, imputed righteousness. Human striving is insufficient and righteousness is a gift from God, but through the inner disciplines we can participate with God receiving grace for transformation.

Richard Foster's classic text, *Celebration of Discipline* provides a contemporary lens through which to encounter the love of God in the practice of personal piety. John Wesley and others made a distinction between works of piety and works of charity:

Piety—worship, prayer, praying the psalms, singing, Bible study, fasting...

Charity—feeding the hungry, caring for the poor, working for justice/reform...

Foster uses the metaphor of a long, narrow bridge through a deep cavern with sheer drops on either side. The chasm to the right is moral bankruptcy through human strivings for righteousness. This is a heresy of moralism or works-righteousness. The chasm to the left is moral bankruptcy through the absence of human strivings—heresy of antinomianism. The bridge is the path of the spiritual disciplines leading to inner transformation and healing. The path does not produce the change but places us where the change can occur.

The objective is not simply any growth, but rather fruit, the fruits of holiness. A tremendous amount of growth occurs in a swamp. However, a swamp seldom produces fruit. Therefore, good works or means of grace focus God's work in us, renewing the image of God, and growth in holiness.

Means of grace are an important aspect of our Wesleyan heritage. However, they are not merely a point of historical posterity of an archaic movement. Means of grace are a significant aspect of a vital living tradition. Means of grace are practices, recognized by Christian tradition, that help shape personal and communal faith. They are means by which personal and communal spiritual formation may be formed and cultivated.

John Wesley desired to embody holy living. He felt that the means of grace should be used constantly thus combining the inner with the outer expressions of salvation [and his doctrines of justification and sanctification].

John Wesley defined the means of grace as "the ordinary channels of conveying [God's] grace into the souls of [persons]." Wesley divided the means of grace into two groups: instituted and prudential. The instituted means of grace roughly corresponded to traditional Christian understandings of works of piety, or development of personal holiness, while the prudential means of grace corresponded to traditional Christian understandings of works of mercy or expressions of social holiness. It is important to remember that within the Wesleyan tradition the means of grace, although described separately, are never meant to be understood or practiced separately.

According to John Wesley's "The Scripture Way of Salvation," one of his most often preached sermons and the most comprehensive explanation of his practical theology, works of piety and works of mercy are necessary to a Christian's sanctification. However, these fruits are not necessary in the same sense or in the same degree as faith. According to Wesley, a person may be sanctified without them, but may not be sanctified without faith, and then if there be time and opportunity the fruits become necessary.

The instituted means of grace include prayer, searching the Scriptures, the Lord's Supper, fasting, and Christian conferencing. These are described as works of piety in this sermon. The prudential means of grace are designated works of mercy and described as relating to the bodies and souls of persons such as feeding the hungry; clothing the naked; entertaining the stranger; visiting those who are in prison, sick, or variously afflicted; instructing the seeker; awakening the sinner; quickening the lukewarm; confirming the wavering; comforting the afflicted; succoring the tempted; or contributing in any manner to the saving of souls.

Conclusion

From our earliest roots, Methodism is a movement characterized by intentional and steady growth in grace most often in small group settings. Through small groups, complemented by field preaching, Methodists participated in Christian practices, both individually and together, to receive and share God's grace. Notably, one of our doctrinal resources, the General Rules, offers guidance on nurturing faith together in small groups through practicing the means of grace. In the spirit of early Methodism, I pray United Methodists will continue to cultivate spaces for small group gatherings. Through practicing the means of grace, individually and together in community, we receive and respond to God's grace in our lives and the world. By welcoming all, Methodists gather to grow in grace encouraging one another as we participate in God's sanctification of us and all creation.

CHAPTER 3
LOCAL AND CONNECTIONAL

The local congregation is most often the primary context for experiencing "church." The local church is where our Christian journey begins and ends; it's where we worship the Triune God and where we participate in God's unfolding work in the world. In United Methodism the local church not only gathers individuals to worship God in a specific community but also connects to a network of conferences to participate in God's mission in the world. In chapter 2, we explored the very important role of small groups and practicing means of grace in the early Methodist renewal movement and today. This chapter focuses on the local church, the primary place for preaching and worship. We reflect on how and why we gather in local congregations and participate in United Methodist connectionalism through itineracy and conferences—to share God's love and grace by participating in God's unfolding work in the world.

Local Church

The local church is the primary place where we come together in worship each week, study the Scriptures, and share in the Lord's Supper. From our local churches we embark on journeys of outreach and ministry with neighbors near and far. It's through the waters of the baptismal font in the front corner of our church where children and loved ones are initiated into the body of Christ and incorporated into God's ongoing mission. Young couples walk the aisles of our church as they make a new covenant in marriage together, while others, after many years of beautiful and challenging life together, mourn the death of their loved ones. The local church in its many embodiments—of various sizes, architectural and worship styles, and range of facilities—is a place where we encounter and worship God together as a community of believers.

The local church as experienced by most United Methodists is a relatively recent development. During the eighteenth-century early Methodist renewal movement within the Church of England, Methodists participated in small groups where they experienced transformative grace and moved toward holiness together, as we discussed in chapter 2. Modeled on religious societies within the Church of England organized through the Society for Promoting Christian Knowledge, these small groups populated a network of circuits eventually stretching across the British Isles.

John Wesley developed leaders, lay and clergy, to nurture and oversee the growth of the movement in these small groups. Leadership roles facilitated by the Wesleys included class and band leaders, exhorters, stewards/trustees, nurses, teachers, and preachers. As the movement matured later in the eighteenth century and then following John Wesley's death, Methodists gathered in more ecclesial spaces referred to as "chapels," always careful to distinguish their Nonconformist (the official name for recognized denominations outside the state church) gatherings from "churches" within the Church of England. These settings resembled small modest churches in villages and towns. This was also the case in North America. Under the influence and guidance of Bishop Francis Asbury, itinerant and local preachers were also assigned to care for the expanding movement in North America. Local preachers lived in communities and provided consistent pastoral care and nurture for small groups, while the itinerant preachers traveled the circuits presiding at the Lord's Supper. In this way, the local church as a space for worship, sacraments, discipleship, and outreach cared for by an ordained elder, and in some cases full-time staff, is a somewhat recent development in Methodism.

The language of "local church" came into use within Methodism in the United States by the 1920s. However, before this description became the norm, Methodist congregations were referred to as "local societies" as recently as 1904, and the language of society was common in all branches of Methodism until 1939. In 1944 the section previously described as "Church Membership" in *The Book of Discipline* was revised and renamed "Local Church." This revised and expanded section describes the local church "as a society of persons who have professed their faith and have joined together in the fellowship of a Christian congregation in order to pray together, to receive the word of exhortation, and watch over one another in love, that they may help each other to work out their salvation."

Although the annual conference continues to be the "official" basic organizational unit within Methodism since 1940 (and arguably functioned in this way since the Wesleys' eighteenth-century renewal movement), following the 1939 union the local church plays the most significant role within our experience. The description or definition of the "local church" included in the *Discipline* may seem familiar in that it echoes themes from United Methodism's mission statement:

The local church provides the most significant arena through which disciple-making occurs. It is a community of true believers under the

Lordship of Christ. It is the redemptive fellowship in which the Word of God is preached by persons divinely called and the sacraments are duly administered according to Christ's own appointment. Under the discipline of the Holy Spirit, the church exists for the maintenance of worship, the edification of believers, and the redemption of the world.[1]

This definition resonates with the denomination's mission statement and is drawn from Scripture, specifically Matthew 28, and tradition, particularly the Articles of Religion and Evangelical United Brethren Confession of Faith—as well as our even older Trinitarian theological roots.

The description of the function of the local church in the following paragraph begins with an orienting statement: "The church of Jesus Christ exists in and for the world." The local church is a "strategic base" from which Christians minister to and with others in society, extending its relationship with the Triune God. "The function of the local church under the guidance of the Holy Spirit is to help people to accept and confess Jesus Christ as Lord and Savior and to live their daily lives in light of their relationship with God."[2] The paragraph then adds the following to the list of the local church's functions: ministering to the surrounding community, providing nurture and training when appropriate, cooperating in ministry with other local churches in ministry, living in ecological responsibility, and participating in the worldwide mission of the church.

Local congregations come in all sizes and shapes, each with their own unique story. The following describes a part of one congregation's story. A British Methodist church called Stapleton was facing a looming challenge. They had dwindled over the years until they were just eight people—and those were the Sundays when everyone could attend. They had done all they knew to do to "reach out to young people" and grow the church, but there they were, still only eight people gathered in worship.

A time finally came when the matriarch, and heart of the congregation, reached an age and situation when she could no longer live alone. She moved into a care facility some distance from the church. The congregation was heartbroken that Muriel would no longer be able to worship with them. Stapleton discussed the situation and finally decided that if they were a dying church anyway, why not have a grand gesture to support Muriel in her new setting. They decided to move their worship every fourth Sunday to the care facility where Muriel resided.

The first Sunday people steadily flowed into the small lobby space. Initially, about fifteen minutes before the small informal service was scheduled to begin there were about a dozen people gathered. A few minutes before the start of the service, a dozen more. There were extended families of church members, also families of residents in the care facility, and former active members who had faded into busy schedules. By the end of the first hymn, approximately sixty people gathered for worship. On the second Sunday the number doubled.

It was not long before the congregation decided to meet regularly at the care facility. They found growth through gathering as the body of Christ beyond the building on to which they tried so desperately to hold. Reaching out to Muriel, her neighbor residents, staff, and their families, who needed not just a place, but a community with whom to worship God, they found new life. By reaching out in selfless love, the kind that only imminent closure freed them to consider, they worshipped the Triune God and participated in the unusual unfolding of God's work.

Worship

When we gather in local churches, most often on Sunday mornings but also throughout the week, we gather to worship the Triune God. All are welcome to share in this worshipful work, since it is at God's invitation that we gather in relationship with God, neighbor, and with all creation. Christian, and Methodist, worship is grounded in Scripture. Through the Holy Spirit and teachings of Scripture, patterns of worship connect to generations of believers. Our Christian worship continues to imitate practices led by Jesus Christ among his disciples and those he encountered. Some aspects of our worship echo the practices of God's covenant people described in the Old Testament. Methodist worship shares patterns with the worldwide body of Christians, while also offering distinctives resulting in a recognizable ethos across United Methodism. And yet, while we share so much in common with Christian siblings across time and space, worship among United Methodists across the world also demonstrates the uniqueness of every local church gathering and even every worship service. Through the Holy Spirit we are unified in grace and truth, and in the Holy Spirit we are granted unique gifts and experiences.

The pattern of worship United Methodists share, often described as Word and Table, can be found in the first few pages of our hymnal. *The United Methodist Book of Worship* and *The United Methodist Hymnal* provide guides and resources to facilitate worship in local churches, conferences, and beyond. They contribute to our connectionalism by providing shared experiences. Both the *Book of Worship* and *Hymnal* are grounded in Scripture and demonstrate Wesleyan doctrinal emphases, especially themes of grace.

Word and Table

United Methodist's basic pattern of worship, often described as Word and Table, is grounded in Scripture and inspired by Jesus's ministry with the earliest disciples. Jesus read and taught from Scripture, God's Word, at the time consisting of only what we refer to as the Old Testament. The accounts of Jesus's ministry and teaching and Paul's letters to emerging

Our Christian worship continues to imitate practices led by Jesus Christ among his disciples and those he encountered.

Christian communities make up most of the New Testament. Jesus also shared meals, especially with his disciples on the night before his crucifixion, called the Lord's Supper. There are numerous examples of Jesus's teaching and sharing meals at tables. When we gather in worship, we resemble these occasions of Word and Table. The primary time for our gathering in worship is Sunday morning, the day and time of Jesus's resurrection. Each Sunday worship is a little Easter.

In worship we receive the Word of God in a number of ways. We hear the Word of God as Scripture read before the sermon. We also hear the Word of God proclaimed in the form of a preacher's sermon focusing on Scriptures read in worship. While not all sermons are preached on texts from one of the four Gospels in the New Testament, every sermon proclaims the gospel of Jesus Christ. In the sermon, whether delivered from a high dramatic pulpit, with screens and audio enhancement, or delivered on the floor in the midst of a small congregation, we receive a message from the Triune God. That message may be directly connected to the words read or preached, a particular phrase, explanation, or illustration. It may also be an indirect experience of the Holy Spirit, a feeling or nudge, as we contemplate God's guidance for our lives of faith in the body of Christ sent to share God's love with the world.

Worship also includes various responses to the proclamation of the Word in its many forms. Appropriate responses to the Word include acts of commitment such as sharing in statements of creed. Creed, meaning belief, originates from the Latin word credo, or "I believe." While personal statements of belief are important, in worship the gathered community makes their statement of belief in unison as a body, the body of Christ. Other responses include the giving of offerings, such as tithes and other gifts, including musical offerings. Among the offerings, usually at least once a month, the bread and grape juice are offered and placed on the altar table in preparation for the Lord's Supper.

While some Christian denominations use wine when sharing the Lord's Supper, United Methodists most often use grape juice. Methodists, including many Methodist women, in the United States and Great Britain provided leadership in the early twentieth century temperance movement that advocated for the prohibition of alcohol. In response to the temperance movement and prohibition, Thomas Welch first pasteurized Concord grape juice in 1869 as an alternative to wine for use in worship services. His son Charles, a Methodist layperson, shared the pasteurized grape juice with other Protestant denominations resulting in the commercial production of Welch's Grape Juice.

The Lord's Supper, Holy Communion, or Eucharist is a special time of gathering within worship in which we remember Jesus Christ's last supper among his disciples before his trial judged by Pilate and death on the cross. To prepare for the Lord's Supper the pastor and congregation pray together the Great Thanksgiving, a prayer shared by all Christians worldwide that echoes Jesus's words at his last supper with the disciples. In this prayer the pastor takes the bread and cup, gives thanks over the bread and cup, breaks the bread, and gives the bread and cup. As Methodists we believe Jesus Christ through the Holy Spirit is present with us in the bread and cup. At the conclusion of the meal the people gathered are sent in ministry with a blessing to all the world.

"A Singing People"

We sing in worship today because as Methodists we have always held song as an essential part of our worship—we even teach and learn our beliefs more often through song than from texts. Singing hymns in communal worship is a moving and formational practice. Singing prayers and hymns with children teaches them and adults alike the simple and beautiful truths of God's love for us and all creation. In the later stages of dementia and Alzheimer's disease, persons demonstrating little to no awareness of their surroundings can seem miraculously present through singing familiar songs from deep in their memories. According to Saint Augustine, to sing is to pray twice. Singing together in community has also been shown to encourage healing, particularly following lockdowns during the COVID-19 global pandemic.

From the earliest days of the renewal movement led by the Wesleys, Methodists have been known as "a singing people." Next to Scripture, Methodist hymnals continue to be one of the most formative resources in the lives of individuals and communities of faith. The current hymnal, published in 1989, provides a range of resources for community worship from hymns and psalms, prayers, and orders of service. The current hymnal provides worship resources from a wide diversity of creators with some stretching over one thousand years of use.

The primary purpose of hymn-singing in the early Methodist renewal movement was Christian formation in Scripture and doctrine. Charles's poetry sung widely as hymns, more than anything, else formed the early Methodists. John Wesley compiled the first hymnbook used in North America in 1737 for use during his ministry in Georgia. In his hymns, both instruments and products of the movement, Charles drew heavily from scripture both in verbal allusions and imagery. In the hymn book of 1780, John's arrangement of hymns was based on a pattern of spiritual experience, which could help guide formation in contexts that had less familiarity with Christian Scripture.

Charles Wesley's poems set to music, often well-loved tunes, contributed significantly to the energy and doctrine of the early Methodist movement, which continues today. *The United Methodist Hymnal* includes numerous hymns by Charles Wesley, each grounded in Scripture and formational for Christians growing in faith. Some claim as much as 85 percent of the Bible may be present in the hymns composed by Charles Wesley. The hymnal is organized around Wesleyan emphases of doctrine, including grace—prevenient, justifying, and sanctifying.

Baptism: By Water and the Spirit

Through baptism and profession of faith persons are initiated not only into a local church, but into the body of Christ. In baptism we accept God's invitation into relationship, grace, and unconditional love. We confess our sins as well as our belief in the Triune God. We then receive our commission to participate in God's mission to share God's love and grace with our words and in our lives. For United Methodists, baptism most often occurs in the form of sprinkling water from a baptismal font during Sunday morning worship. This is not an exclusive requirement, since at times baptism may also take the form of pouring water over the baptized person's head or their full immersion in water.

Through the Baptismal Covenant, or promises made at baptism, persons are called into ministry and participate in Christian formation. Those baptized as infants are invited, when appropriate, to participate in rituals of Confirmation, both a human act of commitment and the gracious action of the Holy Spirit strengthening and empowering discipleship.[3] Echoing the Baptismal Covenant included in the *Book of Worship*, the *Discipline* describes the covenant and promises made:

> When persons unite as professing members with a local United Methodist church, they profess their faith in God, the Father Almighty, maker of heaven and earth; in Jesus Christ his only Son, and in the Holy Spirit. Thus, they make known their desire to live their daily lives as disciples of Jesus Christ. They covenant together with God and with the members of the local church to keep the vows which are a part of the order of confirmation and reception into the Church:
>
> 1. To renounce the spiritual forces of wickedness, reject the evil powers of the world, and repent of their sin;
>
> 2. To accept the freedom and power God gives them to resist evil, injustice, and oppression;

3. To confess Jesus Christ as Savior, put their whole trust in his grace, and promise to serve him as their Lord;

4. To remain faithful members of Christ's holy church and serve as Christ's representatives in the world;

5. To be loyal to Christ through The United Methodist Church and do all in their power to strengthen its ministries;

6. To faithfully participate in its ministries by their prayers, their presence, their gifts, their service, and their witness;

7. To receive and profess the Christian faith as contained in the Scriptures of the Old and New Testaments.[4]

As baptized and professed members of the body of Christ and The United Methodist Church, each member is encouraged in their faith and encouraged to practice their faith in all aspects of life.

Ordained pastors are given the privilege, as well as authority, to preside at the baptism and confirmation of individuals. A related primary responsibility of pastors is for the spiritual well-being of those members and preparation for membership. While the pastor is primarily responsible, the congregation shares in this nurture. Additional guidelines for practices of baptism and confirmation are provided in the *Discipline*. Especially noteworthy is the instruction regarding not re-baptizing.

> No pastor shall re-baptize. The practice of re-baptism does not conform with God's action in baptism and is not consistent with Wesleyan tradition and the historic teaching of the church. Therefore, the pastor should counsel any person seeking re-baptism to participate in the rite of re-affirmation of baptismal vows.[5]

In baptism, we acknowledge God's action in our lives. Though we are responding to God's action, the primary focus of baptism is God's invitation and forgiveness. United Methodists do not re-baptize since

God's action is faithful and unchanging. Instead of practicing re-baptism to rededicate one's promises, the rituals of confirmation and reaffirmation of the baptismal covenant are encouraged.

Often pastors will invite congregations to remember their baptisms each year in January to begin the New Year or perhaps around Easter. It was neither January nor Easter, and our pastor was not planning to invite the congregation to remember our baptism quite yet. My daughter was about two and half years old. As the child of two ordained persons, pastors at heart though appointed to extension ministries, she was used to witnessing long conversations particularly after worship on Sunday mornings.

Not surprisingly, and understandably, her tolerance for long conversations after worship had limits. This one Sunday after worship, both my spouse and I were invited into conversations in two different places in the sanctuary at a distance from the front of the church. On numerous Sundays, Clare would make her way to the front of the church greeting people and exploring, often climbing into the pulpit, perusing the congregational Bible, or sitting under the altar. On this Sunday, she noticed something different for the first time: the baptismal font.

Baptismal fonts typically contain water, usually blessed, making the water technically "holy." Noticing the font, Clare went to investigate. I could see her out of the corner of my eye. I then heard the pastor call Clare's name, asking and guiding at the same time, "Clare, what are you doing? Let's not play in the baptism waters. You could get wet." The pastor's voice was kind and strong. She practices gentle boundaries in the worship space with the children, with much more patience than I could manage. Because of her hospitality, we all felt the welcome of God.

But Clare's unattended toddler hands and the blessed holy water of the baptismal font could be a less than ideal situation. I could see the situation unfolding from the corner of my eye. Before either I or the pastor could get to Clare at the baptismal font, my daughter had constructed a step, ascended, and opened the font revealing the clear and refreshing water representing life in community with the Triune God.

The pastor asked again, still with kindness and an authentic interest, "Clare, what are you doing?" At that point, Clare announced, "I remember my baptism!" And though her hands were small she scooped out the water with surprising generosity for those close by. Clare extended an invitation with infectious joy, "Would you like to remember your baptism too? Remember God loves you!" Though the pastor really is so patient and nurturing with children of all ages, I worried if we were entering a new space of possible tension. The pastor received most of the baptismal remembrance soaking her hair and alb along with several other adults and children. After gasps, and a profound silence, fortunately, there were squeals, smiles, and water all around. The pastor affirmed Clare and all of us basking in the joy of remembering our identities in God's family, baptized by water in the Spirit. The next Sunday in worship, the pastor led us to remember our baptisms, which is no longer only an annual occasion.

Church Membership

According to the *Discipline*, "The membership of a local UMC shall include all people who have been baptized and all people who have professed their faith."[6] Both baptized and professing members of any local United Methodist church are members of both the worldwide United Methodist connection and members of the church universal. The *baptized membership* "of a local United Methodist church shall include all baptized people who have received Christian baptism in the local congregation or elsewhere, or whose membership has been transferred to the local United Methodist Church subsequent to baptism in some other congregation." *Professing members* of a local United Methodist church "shall include all baptized people who have come into membership by profession of faith through appropriate services of the baptismal covenant in the ritual or by transfer from other churches." The *Discipline* goes on to state, "For statistical purposes, church membership is equated to the number of people listed on the roll of professing members."[7]

Membership in The United Methodist Church includes hospitality to those connected to other denominations through Affiliate and Associate Memberships. "A professing member of The United Methodist Church, of an affiliated autonomous Methodist or united church or of a Methodist church that has a concordat agreement with The United Methodist Church, who resides for an extended period in a city or community at a distance from the member's home church may on request be enrolled as an *affiliate member* of a United Methodist Church located in the vicinity of the temporary residence." Affiliate members may participate in fellowship, receive pastoral care, and hold an office, though not one that allows a vote in a United Methodist body beyond the local church. Affiliate members are counted as members of their home church only. "A member of another denomination may become an *associate member* under the same conditions, but may not become a voting member of the church council."[8] The number of membership categories within the local church attempts to maintain continuity with our early Methodist tradition as well as provide opportunities for individuals to express their Christian faith and discipleship in its many embodiments.

The function and purpose of the local church is structured to facilitate participation in the broader church's mission, both locally as well as through the connectional structure. The local church, also known as a charge in Methodist tradition, connects to the annual conference through a charge conference. At a charge conference the district superintendent or another representative of the annual conference presides to worship, appoint leadership, make important decisions, and celebrate ministry in connection. The following section will discuss conference gatherings. Conferences in their various forms continue to facilitate the broader church's mission to make disciples for the transformation of the world.

Conference as Connection

Many of the means of grace that we talked about before are likely not too surprising: prayer, fasting, the Lord's Supper, visiting the sick and feeding hungry people. But John Wesley added another means to the practices kept by Methodists, one that defines the very nature of life in the local church and Methodist small groups. In the Wesleyan tradition, conferencing remains a means of grace since it is a significant gathering for our experience in Christian community as United Methodists. Beginning with John Wesley's leadership, gathering for worship, fellowship, and planning the work of ministry was a means to receive and to share God's grace. As the early Methodist movement spread across the British Isles and increased in numbers, Wesley gathered the preachers in conference. These gatherings demonstrated and embodied the interrelated spiritual and operational dynamics of the connection that facilitated the ministry of the early Methodist movement. In our strongest and most faithful moments, United Methodism gathers to practice conferencing and embody our connectionalism.

Most, if not all, of the Methodist and Wesleyan traditions across the world continue to practice forms of conferencing. In The United Methodist Church conferencing is embodied in both time and place—in bodies that meet at regular intervals from specific regions. United Methodism consists of a structure of conferences with interrelated accountability (charge, annual, district, jurisdictional/central, and general) and support that visibly represents connection and guides the ministry of the church.

In recent years pressure upon conference structures has increased. For United Methodism, declining membership mainly in the United States and Europe presents a need to consolidate bureaucratic structures, particularly within and between district and annual conferences, restructuring to enhance efficiencies. In other parts of the world, particularly in

Africa, increasing membership presents a different set of issues requiring expanded support structures, including additional annual conferences within central conferences, to facilitate the ministry of the church.

The most authoritative body in The United Methodist Church is the General Conference. Next in the connectional organization are jurisdictional conferences—of which there are five in the United States—and numerous central conferences in regions around the world—which carry out delegated duties from the general conference. Jurisdictional and central conferences mediate between the general conference and annual conferences. In the United States, district conferences support the annual conference and missionary annual conferences, connecting it with local congregations, which are also organized into charge conferences.

Within United Methodism, the General Conference is the authoritative body and voice. It is the only entity with authority to speak for the denomination. Typically, the General Conference meets every four years, or quadrennium, and consists of elected delegates from each annual conference across the denomination. Bishops preside at General Conference sessions, having voice but no vote. The General Conference last met for a regular session in 2016, followed by a special session called by the Council of Bishops in 2019. Because of the COVID-19 global pandemic the next meeting of the General Conference is in 2024.

The General Conference is a legislative body consisting of more than a dozen committees that bring legislation to the plenary for consideration. Approved legislation appears in *The Book of Discipline*, which is published following each regular session of General Conference. Any United Methodist may submit a petition to General Conference for consideration. The General Conference also considers resolutions for inclusion in *The Book of Resolutions* also published following each General Conference regular session. The General Conference usually meets quadrennially in late spring followed by the jurisdictional conferences in July.

Within United Methodism, the General Conference is the authoritative body and voice. It is the only entity with authority to speak for the denomination.

Jurisdictional conferences, like the General Conference, usually meet every four years within a month or two following General Conference. Jurisdictions meet in their regions, but simultaneously with other jurisdictional conferences. The jurisdictional, like General, conference also consists of delegates elected from annual conferences. Jurisdictional and central conferences perform two main responsibilities: electing episcopal leaders and setting conference boundaries. Central conferences are very similar to jurisdictional conferences but exist outside the United States. In preparation for General Conference 2024, legislation was submitted to revise this structure for the purpose of practicing greater parity and recovering from the systemic sins of colonialism.

The annual conference, both currently and historically, is the basic organizational unit of the denomination. The annual conference connects local churches with the broader governing structure to facilitate participation in the mission of the church. Annual conferences are also organized into districts to facilitate ministry and fellowship, though districts are not granted significant authority within the structure. While baptized persons hold membership in local churches, persons receiving ordination in The United Methodist Church hold membership in the annual conference. Similar to General, jurisdictional, and central conferences, annual conference delegates consist of an equal number of clergy and laity. Since early Methodism and John Wesley's leadership, annual conferences are an opportunity to gather in worship, fellowship, and planning for ministry. Many describe annual conferences as family reunions.

Conferences remain the most significant connectional structures and gatherings within United Methodism. Conferences provide a thoughtful and agile structure for an international connection. As United Methodism continues to shift, this structure may experience even more opportunity to reflect the growing vitality of its witness and mission in international contexts.

Itineracy

Itineracy is a distinctive characteristic of Methodism initiated by John Wesley in the British context and continued by Francis Asbury in North America. John Wesley facilitated itinerant ministry, the sending of preachers to visit a series of local congregations, to provide spiritual leadership and care particularly where the Church of England was not strong. In early North American Methodism itinerant preachers, usually ordained persons, also provided the sacraments to communities. Itineracy today is a form of traveling ministry, directed by bishops and implemented by district superintendents, that allows for exchange of pastoral leadership and resources across the connection. Asbury, Coke, and their nineteenth-century episcopal descendants exercised substantial authority in the appointment of itinerant preachers. In the twentieth century, episcopal leadership, though still authoritative, shared the more complex responsibility of appointment-making with district superintendents. The practice of consultation in appointment-making emerged as a significant revision to itinerant ministry in recent years.

Beginning with John Wesley himself, itineracy grew from a desire to meet the greatest needs and a willingness to travel to address those needs. Itineracy eventually came to carry the momentum of the movement's mission to spread scriptural holiness over the land. In Wesley's British Methodism, itineracy can be seen as a pragmatic embodiment of the movement's missional and connectional character that helped maintain doctrinal integrity. Flexible and mainly resilient in diverse geographies over the centuries, itinerancy effectively established Methodism in the United States. Today the willingness to move still remains at the heart of Methodism's identity and purpose.

Itinerating preachers manifested "the connexion" Wesley worked so diligently to establish and sustain. In early Methodism under Wesley's leadership, the connection was sustained by his authority to appoint itinerating preachers (after his death the conference inherited his authority). Through a clause included in the deed of every preaching house within the Methodist connection, Wesley maintained this authority. The clause stipulates the obligation of the trustees of the preaching house to accept preachers approved and appointed by Wesley. This clause helped ensure the trustees could not refuse these preachers.

Alternatively, the trustees were entrusted with holding their preachers accountable to acceptable doctrine, in early Methodism described as "no other doctrine than that contained in Mr. Wesley's *Notes upon the New Testament* and four volumes of *Sermons*."[9] This shared practice and preservation of doctrinal consistency continues in the use of the trust clause and relationship to current doctrinal materials in the deeds of United Methodist facilities.

Preachers itinerated frequently in early Methodism. Initially preachers itinerated to a new circuit at least every three months; at most one might stay as long as two years. The basic issue concerning the itineracy of full-time preachers was not that the preachers needed to move at particular intervals, but rather their sincerity of commitment to Methodism's mission. For Wesley this was demonstrated by their willingness to move as needed.

Francis Asbury continued Wesley's emphasis upon frequent itineracy of full-time preachers, though he experienced some dissent from other early Methodist leaders in the United States. Thomas Coke and Asbury explained itineracy with language that "everything is kept moving as far as possible."[10] They cited biblical foundations and described itineracy as "the primitive and apostolic plan"[11] after Wesley's example. This peculiar Methodist polity, which complemented the local preachers, provided an incredibly effective method of expansion and fulfillment of Wesley's missional vision, planting Methodism not only across the ocean but also across the frontier.

A guiding principle of itineracy within United Methodism is its *openness*. This means appointments are made without regard to race, ethnic origin, gender, color, disability, marital status, or age. Open itineracy is practiced in partnership between bishops and district superintendents, pastors, and congregations. According to the *Discipline*, annual conferences provide training for Staff/Pastor-Parish Relations Committees to "prepare congregations to receive the gifts and graces of appointed clergy without regard to race, ethnic origin, gender, color, disability, marital status, or age."[12] Open itineracy is a historic value held by United Methodism and its predecessor traditions. According to the *Discipline*: "The United Methodist Church promotes and holds in high esteem the opportunity of an inclusive church...with the formation of open itineracy."[13]

John Wesley encouraged the preaching of laity and women with extraordinary calls and gifts, though he did not directly challenge the policies of the Church of England. Francis Asbury encouraged the liberation of enslaved persons as well as the ministries of Richard Allen and other pastors and laity of African American descent. Throughout Methodism's history, prophetic moments demonstrate our commitment to God's unfolding reign.

Structured for Service

There is a profound simplicity in the early Methodist movement's purpose. The Wesleys were less concerned with doctrinal disagreements than with an imperative to share and live the gospel of Jesus Christ. This is to say difficulties of organization as well as availability of resources and leadership will persist. However, our Methodist heritage offers helpful guidance for continued response to God's calling and sending United Methodists to participate in God's reign.

In addition to conferences, a number of councils and agencies function within the structure of The United Methodist Church. These bodies function in distinctive and significant ways to connect and integrate ministries and resources across the denomination. As an introduction to the *Agencies and General Agencies*, the *Discipline* states, "Connectionalism is an important part of our identity as United Methodists."[14] These entities, at their best, provide leadership and contributions to the life of the denomination for the purpose of fulfilling our mission to participate in God's work in the world.

The general agencies may be organized into categories. For example, the Connectional Table and the General Council on Finance and Administration are supervisory councils. Following General Conference in 1972, the four basic program components were identified as General Board of Church and Society—Advocacy; General Board of Discipleship—Nurture; General Board of Global Ministries (including the United Methodist Commission on Relief)—Outreach; and General Board of Higher Education and Ministry—Vocation.

With these four program boards, three other general commissions are listed among them in the *Discipline*: the General Commission on Religion and Race, the General Commission on United Methodist Men, and the General Commission on the Status and Role of Women. Administrative units include the General Board of Pensions, The United Methodist Publishing House, General Commission on Archives and History, General Commission on Communication, Standing Committee on Central Conference Matters, and JUSTPEACE Center for Mediation and Conflict Transformation.

It is important for General Conference as well as jurisdictional conferences, central conferences, and annual conferences to legislate for renewal facilitating the embodiment of our beliefs for the fulfillment of our shared mission. However, renewal seems most often to come from communities of faith—or institutions of faithful—sent by God in Jesus Christ through the Holy Spirit to participate in the reign of God. These communities and institutions exist in a variety of locations, many outside the United States where United Methodism and Christianity experience significant growth in grace and numbers. Our structure facilitates our shared mission for service as United Methodists in a worldwide connection.

Conclusion

In this chapter we reflected on the local church as our primary setting for gathering as United Methodists through local churches related to a worldwide connection of conferences and organizations that facilitate our shared mission and ministry. In worship we hear the Word proclaimed and gather at the Table to share in the Lord's Supper. We baptize with water symbolizing the work of the Holy Spirit in us and among us as members of the body of Christ. As United Methodists we are known for our singing and connection represented in part by an itinerate ministry. Through our connection of conferences and organizations we participate in worldwide witness to the gospel of Jesus Christ. In the next chapter, we will reflect on our rich and varied heritage of social advocacy and Christian mission.

CHAPTER 4
TENACIOUS MISSION

United Methodism continues a long and tenacious heritage of missional impact. The United Methodist Church's Committee on Relief continues to be one of the most respected relief agencies in the world. Alongside the American Red Cross and other secular relief organizations, UMCOR is well known for being one of the first agencies in and among the last to leave catastrophic natural or human-imposed violent disasters. We can speculate about why this is the case—perhaps effective leadership, planning, or strategic use of resources. While these may all be pertinent reasons for UMCOR's remarkable reputation, this distinctive missional impact grows from our Methodist roots.

From its beginnings, the early Methodist movement sought to inspire a renewed imagination for God's transformation in communities. While such transformation often refers to God's grace within individuals through holiness or sanctification, the earliest Methodists did not stop with the inner spiritual life. As Charles and John Wesley gathered with classmates and colleagues in Oxford, they contemplated the impact of the inner spiritual life on their Christian practices and love of neighbor. In contrast to other Christian traditions, Methodism did not begin with a set of beliefs to be defended. Methodism's missional character was innate from the very beginning. The beliefs grew and developed as layers in response to relationships nurtured in small groups and communities as discussed in previous chapters. Through interactions with others and the steady authentic building of relationships, Methodism's missional character continues to grow.

In this chapter we will explore Methodism's legacy of missional impact, beginning with works of charity and empowerment in and beyond small groups in early Methodism. John Wesley and early Methodists created initiatives for accessibility to microfinance, health care, and education. Building on a strong economic ethic from John Wesley and the early Methodists, Methodists in the United States established numerous hospitals and institutions of higher education. Methodists resisted slavery, including all in their small groups and ministry. Methodists also affirmed the gifts of women, ordaining the first woman in the United States. While there is always more to learn and ways to grow in God's sanctification, Methodists continue to demonstrate significant advocacy for social justice.

Redeeming Relationships: "No Holiness but Social Holiness"

Methodism's heritage of mission and social advocacy grows from John Wesley's emphasis upon the Holy Spirit's work of sanctification in persons—and communities. The familiar quote from Wesley, "no holiness but social holiness," does not refer to the importance of justice as a component of the Christian gospel, but to the essential nature of Christianity as a social faith requiring relationship with others. The following quote from John Wesley's preface to his *Hymns and Sacred Poems* written in 1739 includes more context: "Directly opposite to this is the gospel of Christ. Solitary religion is not to be found there.

'Holy solitaries' is a phrase no more consistent with the gospel than holy adulterers. The gospel of Christ knows of no religion but social; no holiness but social holiness."

While extraordinary stories exist of individuals coming to and being sustained in Christian faith as solitary beings, this is very rare. As Wesley and the early Methodists realized, Christian faith, love of God and love of neighbor, is most fruitfully practiced in relationships within communities of faith. Through nurturing accountable relationships Methodism grew deeply in persons and expanded broadly through communities to share God's love in Jesus Christ through the Holy Spirit.

The Holy Club, Oxford

As young adults in Oxford, John and Charles with their friends gathered in small groups to attend Eucharist, pray, fast, study Scripture, and encourage one another in Christian discipleship. A significant component of that encouragement was accountability and prayer to facilitate love of neighbor among their friends, but also among those they encountered in need of God's love. At the urging of William Morgan, an early Oxford Methodist, practicing Christian faith included daily action showing love and care to orphaned children as well as infirm, impoverished, and incarcerated persons. In 1731 John describes a weekly ritual of visiting the poorest children in Oxford each Wednesday. The Oxford Methodists eventually employed someone to care for these children. John Wesley also preached once a month in the Castle Prison at Oxford, and members of the Holy Club, or early Oxford Methodists, visited the prison daily, some members visiting twice per week. Through relationships with other believers as well as neighbors, some in need, early Methodists in Oxford experienced and participated in God's redeeming work in and through them.

The New Room, Bristol

A second example of early Methodist missional impact growing from relationships among small groups is the New Room, located in Bristol, England. (It is actually the oldest Methodist building in the world despite its description as "New.") In early 1739, members from two Methodist small groups in Bristol approached John Wesley about building a gathering space in which the groups could meet. The New Room opened in May 1739. While the meeting house provided space for small groups to gather for study and worship, it also offered a base for missional outreach. Methodists connected to the New Room organized a soup kitchen to provide food for impoverished neighbors, a school for children without accessibility to education, as well as clothes and medical care at no cost. The New Room also served as a base for ministry with the incarcerated in a nearby prison. Coincidentally, John Wesley's often quoted line from the preface to *Hymns and Sacred Poems* was written the same year as the New Room's opening in 1739: "The gospel of Christ knows of no religion but social; no holiness but social holiness."[1]

The upper level of the New Room provided rooms for hospitality, a small theological library, and classrooms for instruction of preachers. The upper level contained approximately twelve rooms designed around an octagonal cupola including windows looking down into the worship space. Some of the upper rooms served as accommodations for traveling Methodist preachers, while others hosted a modest theological library used by preachers and small groups. Preachers, usually laypersons not credentialed by the Church of England, received instruction from John Wesley and others in theological and pastoral matters as well as feedback on their preaching and worship leadership. Through the cupola windows the instructor could survey the worship space below, including a view of the preacher delivering a sermon as well as the congregation receiving that sermon.

Interestingly, small groups in Bristol offered a model for early Methodist fundraising. The small groups collected money, also referred to as subscriptions, to support the building of the New Room and its subsequent ministries. Each small group participant committed to donating regularly, no matter how small the amount, to cover costs and meet needs. This fundraising strategy managed pressure on already economically stretched participants by leveraging the resources of more affluent participants who covered the donations of any unable to contribute.

The Foundery, London

The Foundery Society in London was organized in April 1740. The Foundery was a site for deliberations for early Methodists about their governance; it was also known as a site for innovative Christian outreach in the midst of complex systems of poverty in London. Previously an armory, the facilities were relatively expansive, providing seating for fifteen hundred as well as rooms for teaching, ministry, and accommodations. While an active Methodist site from 1739–85, most of the activities were eventually moved to a larger and more fitting facility, City Road Chapel, later in the century. John Wesley conducted several experiments in outreach from the Foundery, including a lending stock, poorhouses, and a medical dispensary. These demonstrated Wesley's pastoral wisdom and innovation to treat both symptoms and systems of poverty, empowering many Methodists not merely to survive, but to live sustainably and even flourish.

In the early decades of the Methodist renewal movement many of those attracted to the classes and band meetings were economically poor. For many of the earliest decades of Methodism, the majority of participants were not only poor but they were also mostly women, youth, and young adults. In the later decades of the eighteenth century following the movement's consolidation, those active in the movement represented in greater numbers the middle classes, possibly demonstrating a long-term effectiveness of such programs and the support of new institutional contexts.

Wesley had hoped that the Methodist movement would eventually "have all things common," meaning participants would share their possessions after the example of early Christians described in the Book of Acts. This proved difficult to coordinate and was increasingly complicated as the movement grew. In 1746, Wesley experimented with a different economic program of assistance: the lending stock, a microloan program funded by a collection among Wesley's more affluent friends in London. Two stewards were appointed from the society to hold the fifty pounds collected for disbursement in no- or low-interest loans up to twenty shillings (one British pound) each at the Foundery every Tuesday morning. The microloans could be used for financial relief, but they could also be used to assist small business owners/managers. The loans were granted to members of Methodist small groups who agreed to repay the loan within three months. In the first year, the lending stock assisted 250 people.

Wesley also implemented services for those in need of charity and relief such as "feeble, aged widows" through the establishment of a "poorhouse," a term used in the eighteenth century. These houses provided very simple living spaces for those without access to regular income. The accommodations, also called alms houses, since they were supported by alms or donations, did not receive steady support. The Foundery's residences, consisting of two small houses nearby, hosted approximately twelve people at a time. In the early years following their establishment, the residents included a visually impaired woman and two orphaned children. When in London, Wesley and the preachers visited and shared meals regularly with these neighbors.

"Give All You Can":
Early Methodist Practices
of Wealth-sharing

After the theme of love—both of God and neighbor—the Bible next talks most about money. By some counts, Scripture offers approximately 500 verses on prayer, less than 500 on faith, and 2,350 on money and possessions. Jesus talked extensively about money and possessions, with up to 15 percent of the Gospels and sixteen of Jesus's thirty-eight parables speaking on the use of money.

Numerous contemporary studies of charitable, including church, giving are available. Generally, they each communicate one clear message: in the United States, giving to churches has declined steadily with the decline of memberships over the last several decades.

As wealth has increased in the United States, giving as a percentage of total income has declined. Some point to our increasingly individualistic and consumer-driven landscape, where community responsibility, the common good, and self-sacrifice and community responsibility have become less popular. However, across United Methodism giving continues. According to UM Communications, in 2018 United Methodists gave more than $6.3 billion.[2] The following section reflects on our early Methodist roots that continue to shape practices of generosity today.

It is important to recognize that the context of the early Methodist renewal movement was not entirely different from that of contemporary Protestantism in the United States. While the majority of Methodists were relatively poor, the Wesleys led and taught during the dawning of capitalism in a time when England's colonial trade was flourishing. John consistently addressed issues of poverty, wealth, and benevolence in his writing. Following scriptural themes, he encouraged generosity among Methodists of every socioeconomic class.

After the theme of love—both of God and neighbor—the Bible next talks most about money. By some counts, Scripture offers approximately 500 verses on prayer, less than 500 on faith, and 2,350 on money and possessions.

John was not interested in providing a systematized outline of his own economic ethic. However, Randy Maddox highlights four cornerstones of John's message about wealth and possessions based on repeated themes found in Wesley's writings: (1) the source of all things is God and so all things belong to God, (2) earthly wealth has been placed in human hands to be stewarded on God's behalf, (3) God expects that we use what we are given to provide for our own necessities and then the necessities of others, and (4) to spend our God-given resources on luxuries while others are in need of necessities is to misuse what God has given us.[3]

In his sermon "The Use of Money," John outlined the proper Christian approach toward wealth in what became a famous and often abbreviated quote, "Gain all you can, without hurting either yourself or your neighbour.... Save all you can, by cutting off every expense which serves only to indulge foolish desire.... Give all you can, or in other words give all you have to God." This is not, as is sometimes claimed, an endorsement for the laissez-faire capitalism introduced by Adam Smith. John's writings on similar economic themes, such as *Thoughts on the Scarcity of Provisions* (1773), were contemporary with Smith's *The Wealth of Nations* (1776). However, John Wesley and Adam Smith articulated different ultimate goals concerning economics.

John encouraged the gaining of wealth so that it could be shared among the kingdom of God. Smith advocated the retention of wealth as the basic means of accumulating more wealth. In Wesley's sermon "The Use of Money," the first two points align with Smith's advice for individuals to acquire capital—make all you can and save all you can. Wesley and Smith agree even on the third point, that wealth must be used to the best advantage after it has been acquired. However, John turned this budding economic theory on its head with his last instruction to give all one can. For John, the best use of wealth is to meet the basic needs of one's neighbor—not, as Smith advised, as a tool to acquire more wealth.

In a world where the rich get richer, Wesley admonished excess accumulation as theft from God. In his sermon "On the Danger of Increasing Riches," John Wesley admonishes,

> Do not you know that God entrusted you with that money (all above what buys necessaries for your families) to feed the hungry, to clothe the naked, to help the stranger, the widow, the fatherless; and indeed, as far as it will go, to relieve the wants of all [hu]mankind. How can you, how dare you, defraud your Lord by applying it to any other purpose!

Wesley had a strict definition of wealth that can be found in this sermon. In sum, if anyone held goods above the necessities, one was rich. Wesley applied this definition with unyielding strictness, accusing those who accumulated wealth as stealing from the poor.

The Methodist renewal movement sought various opportunities to demonstrate love of neighbor, including charity schools, orphanages, medical clinics, shelters, meals, zero-interest loans, and other programs to help people meet their most basic needs and to improve their condition. As we have noted, Methodist missional efforts for assisting under-resourced persons initially focused on those within the Methodist small groups. These efforts did not expand to persons beyond the Methodist movement until much later, around the 1780s, through Stranger's Friend Societies.

Continuing to emphasize community, Wesley encouraged wealthy patrons not only to give money to the poor but also to become personally involved, to participate in redeeming relationships. One such patron was Miss March, who had apprehensions about having physical contact and conversation with poor persons. Wesley empathized with her objections but urged her to make such connections after the example of Christ. In his letter to Miss March Wesley asked her to:

> *visit the poor, the widow, the sick, the fatherless, in their affliction.* And this although they should have nothing to recommend them but that

they are bought with the blood of Christ. It is true this is not pleasing to flesh and blood. There are a thousand circumstances usually attending it which shock the delicacy of our nature, or rather of our education. But yet the blessing which follows this labour of love will more than balance the cross.[4]

Giving to those in need was a deep spiritual discipline that brought spiritual benefit to the giver as well as the receiver. Redeeming relationships in Methodism facilitated the sanctification of the giver and the recipient of material resources.

Wealthy and poor people alike were expected to participate in disciplines of sharing material resources—or works of charity and mercy. In this way John Wesley universalized the response to poverty. All were expected to help, including the poor themselves, including the widow with her mites. Wesley insisted upon strict financial discipline—which is one reason, maybe the primary reason, why Methodism did not attract a larger membership during his lifetime. However, John was more interested in renewal through spreading scriptural holiness than large numbers.

This strictness was relaxed after Wesley died. Even before his death, by the 1760s, Wesley softened his own stance and indicated that accumulating a bit of wealth, beyond just the necessities of life, was acceptable as long as it was not the primary goal. And there is a clear correlation between the relaxing of expectations, especially those related to money and wealth, and the growth of Methodist membership.

Primitive Physic: Saving Bodies and Souls

John Wesley pursued a lifelong interest in medicine demonstrated in part by his publication *Primitive Physick* or *An Easy and Natural Method of Curing Most Diseases.* He published the text anonymously in 1747, eventually putting his name to it as author in 1760. Skeptical of the effectiveness of physicians, and most likely moved by those too poor to gain access to medical care, he began stocking and dispensing medicines at several of the preaching houses.

Consulting with those trained in the field, he engaged a surgeon and an apothecary to help him late in 1746 to implement a regular system of dispensing medicine at the Foundery each Friday. In December 1746, the Foundery became a medical dispensary in accord with Wesley's intention of "giving physic to the poor," and treating those with chronic rather than acute illnesses. Following Wesley's announcement, the Foundery's medical dispensary soon grew to a steady monthly clientele of approximately one hundred visitors at an annual cost of less than 120 pounds. When treatments were effective in relieving some ailments, Wesley was quick to refer to God's work in all things. Unlike the lending stock, medical dispensary services were not limited to members of the Foundery Society. Similar medical dispensaries were also generally provided at the preaching houses in Bristol and Newcastle.

In the 1880s Methodism in the United States began a steady pattern of founding hospitals with the first in Brooklyn, New York. Some claim the ambitious Methodist vision for establishing hospitals was inspired by the legacy of Catholics and Episcopalians, as well as Judaism, to provide health care facilities in the nineteenth century. Through a series of efforts over a period of ten years, the Methodist Episcopal Hospital in Brooklyn opened in December 1887. Methodists in other cities replicated this effort: Chicago 1888; Cincinnati 1889; Omaha 1891; Kansas City, Minneapolis, and Philadelphia 1892; Washington, DC 1894; Louisville 1895; Boston 1896; Spokane 1898; and Indianapolis 1899. Southern Methodists followed in the early twentieth century beginning in Atlanta, 1905, St. Louis 1914, Memphis 1921, Houston 1922, Dallas 1927, and Durham, NC 1930. Despite the enormity of the work in challenging times, the Methodists persevered to recover a heritage of care for bodies as well as souls. Methodists opened seventy-five hospitals and clinics by the 1920s. These institutions provided care, including dispensing medicines, for persons of any faith and ability to pay, or no faith and inability to pay for care. Initially, Methodists also participated in the organization of boards to create and reach standards increasing quality of care.[5]

Deaconess orders also emerged in the 1880s with Lucy Rider Meyer establishing the Chicago Training School for City, Home, and Foreign Missions in 1885. The Methodist Episcopal General Conference recognized an order of deaconesses in 1888. Meyer, who had received medical training, provided much of the energy behind the movement and included training for nurses and evangelists. Deaconesses served in many of the early Methodist hospitals across the United States, including Cincinnati, Boston, Chicago, and Washington, DC.[6]

Today, this heritage continues with United Methodists supporting more than 32 million people in over 1,550 communities across the United States through 52 hospitals and health care systems, 105 community service ministries, and 152 older adult ministries.

Education

Beginning in 1739, Wesley carried out the plan George Whitefield had initially conceived of building a school for the coal mining families of Kingswood, holding together knowledge and vital piety in the early Methodist renewal movement. The school included a large preaching hall and facilities for school administrators near Bristol. Scholars of all ages were welcome. In 1748 a new Kingswood school was opened closer to Bath, still near Bristol. Wesley influenced the details of the rules as well as the curriculum, which instructed children on topics from the alphabet to preparation for ministry. Subjects included reading, writing, arithmetic, French, Latin, Greek, Hebrew, rhetoric, geography, chronology, history, logic, ethics, physics, geometry, algebra, and music. Wesley wrote grammars for the English and other language courses and claimed that upon completing the Kingswood curriculum a student would be a better scholar than 90 percent of those completing degrees at Oxford and Cambridge.

Alongside his contributions to the Kingswood School's curriculum, Wesley also compiled the Christian Library for the education of Methodists and its preachers. Begun in 1749, he completed the extensive publishing project in 1755, largely at his own expense. The Christian Library made accessible "extracts from, and abridgements of, the choicest pieces of practical divinity which have been published in the English tongue." Consisting of fifty volumes arranged chronologically from the Early Church, the project was meant to give readers access to the most eminent authors and works of Christian tradition. The Christian Library provided resources for what would become the Course of Study School in 1816 for preachers without access to formal higher education. For over two hundred years the Course of Study has prepared licensed local pastors for ministry.

Methodists established numerous higher education institutions including colleges and universities. Cokesbury College, the first Methodist college in the United States, was built in 1787. Early Methodist colleges include Wesleyan, Randolph-Macon, Dickinson, Allegheny, Emory, Emory and Henry, Ohio Wesleyan, as well as Northwestern, Trinity, and Wofford. The 1820 General Conference encouraged annual conferences to establish colleges. Thirteen were established between 1822 and 1844. By 1880 there were 44 Methodist colleges and universities as well as 11 theological schools, and 130 secondary schools. Today, United Methodists support 95 colleges and universities.

Methodist theological schools or seminaries emerged beginning in 1839 with Newbury Biblical Institute. In 1867 Newbury moved and later became a part of Boston Theological School, which eventually became Boston University. In 1853 Garrett Biblical Institute was established by a financial gift from Eliza Garrett, the widow of the mayor of Chicago. John Dempster convinced her to donate a significant sum of money for theological education. Land in Evanston was purchased near the proposed site of Northwestern University. Barbara Heck Hall, named for one of the first Methodists in the United States, was one of the first buildings. In 1934, Garrett Biblical Institute combined with the Chicago Training School, which was founded in 1885 for the training of women missionaries and deaconesses. Other seminaries followed, including Drew in 1864, Vanderbilt in 1875, Candler at Emory in 1894, and Southern Methodist University in 1908. Today, United Methodism supports thirteen theological schools in the United States.

The University Senate of The United Methodist Church is one of the oldest accrediting bodies in the nation, dating to the General Conference of 1892. The University Senate continues the aspirations of John and Charles Wesley, Francis Asbury, and Thomas Coke to provide quality higher education as an aspect of the ministry of United Methodism and its predecessors in the spirit of the well-known hymn line:

Unite the pair so long disjoin'd
Knowledge and vital piety[7]

The University Senate supports the mission of seminaries and graduate schools of theology whose degrees provide credentials for pastors and practitioners in the church. The University Senate also supports the mission and work of undergraduate institutions. The University Senate encourages accountability guidelines for church-related institutions. The United Methodist Church facilitates over one hundred institutions of higher education, more than any other Protestant denomination.

Holy Tenacity:
Advocacy for God's Work

John Wesley described himself as tenacious when he wrote in his journal in the spring of 1739. As mentioned in the introduction, Wesley's journal entry responded to George Whitefield's field-preaching as the small groups and mission work were also getting started in Bristol:

> [I was] so tenacious of every point relating to decency and order that I should have thought the saving of souls almost a sin if it had not been done in a church.[8]

John Wesley's remarks remind me of the importance of taking risks, even uncomfortable ones as we follow Christ's example to love God and neighbor. The Holy Spirit often guides us into unexpected places to serve the world in surprising and powerful ways. Rather than a tenacious maintenance of decency and order, Methodists share a rich legacy of practicing holy tenacity by participating in God's redemptive work in the world.

Methodists and Racial Equality

John Wesley and early Methodists practiced racial equality in the midst of violent and insidious racial injustice. Wesley encouraged the Christian faith and ministry of numerous persons of African descent. The last letter John Wesley wrote before his death was to William Wilberforce, a well-known British politician and advocate for abolition. The letter communicated words of encouragement to Wilberforce and emphasized the importance of his cause to abolish slavery. Wesley wrote to Wilberforce on February 24, 1791, "Go on, in the name of God and in the power of his might, till even American slavery (the vilest that ever saw the sun) shall vanish away before it."[9]

Early Methodist views on the enslavement of persons in the United States were characterized by Wesley's strong antislavery position, which Francis Asbury and Thomas Coke echoed. Early Methodist conference actions provided a blanket denunciation of slavery. Owners of enslaved persons were not permitted to participate in or lead Methodist small groups or to serve in pastoral leadership. Sadly, over time these clear expectations shifted, creating exceptions, particularly in the South, leading up to the

Civil War. Methodists continue a legacy of working toward racial equality through mission impact as well as inclusion in Methodist communities and political advocacy. From its beginnings, Methodists in the United States advocated for equality by confronting owners of enslaved persons, welcoming persons of American descent in small groups and congregations, as well as petitioning Congress for more just legal actions.

Today The United Methodist Church facilitates the voices of numerous caucus groups advocating for underrepresented persons on the basis of race and gender including African American, Asian American, Latinx/Hispanic, and Native American. In 2000 the General Conference adopted the "Act of Repentance for Racism," which facilitates practices of lament and repentance for the church's participation in racism and inequality across generations. While Methodists continue to practice love of God and neighbor in remarkable ways, as human beings we all have more to learn and need for growth as we participate in God's sanctification of us and the world.

Methodists and Gender Equality

John Wesley and Methodists supported women's leadership in church settings. United Methodists continue to support the ordination of women, which was formally adopted by the Methodist Church's General Conference in 1956. Distinctive among Christian traditions, alongside Quakers and other smaller Christian communities, early Methodism maintained a space for women to preach and lead within the movement. In early British Methodism, women assumed numerous roles from preacher, leader of classes and bands, sick visitor, nurse, prayer leader, Sunday school teacher, and school operator. This support for women's roles and contributions carried into American Methodism. Indeed, Antoinette Brown Blackwell (1825–1921), the first woman to receive ordination in the United States, was ordained by a Wesleyan minister, the Rev. Luther Lee, in 1853.

As human beings
we all have more
to learn and need
for growth as we
participate in God's
sanctification of us
and the world.

According to scholars studying early Methodism in the United States—particularly in Philadelphia, New York, and Baltimore—women made up the majority of members among Methodist small groups. Barbara Ruckle Heck (1734–1804) is heralded as the Mother of American Methodism, having joined a Methodist society in Ireland in 1752 and later convincing her cousin, Philip Embury, to begin preaching in the fall of 1766 following their immigration to New York. Women enjoyed the mutual community, fellowship, and spiritual formation of the small groups, and from about 1770 to 1815 were appointed as class leaders in the Methodist Episcopal Church.

While there remains room for continued expansion of opportunities for women to share their gifts, each year women assume a greater number of leadership roles within Methodism as ordained ministers, district superintendents, general secretaries of agencies, and bishops. The General Commission on the Status and Role of Women advocates for full participation of women in the total life of The United Methodist Church. Their aim is to help the Methodists recognize every person—clergy and lay, women and men, adults and children—as a full and equal part of God's human family.

Methodists Advocating for Social Justice

In response to social challenges, Methodists formed the Methodist Federation for Social Service (MFSS) in Washington, DC, on December 3–4, 1907. Through this group and its leaders, Methodists participated in and eventually led within the Social Gospel a movement to address social crises active in the early twentieth century. Through the Methodist leadership in the Social Gospel movement, the Social Creed was developed and adopted by the Federal Council of Churches.

Although the MFSS chose to remain unofficial in its relationship to General Conference and the denomination generally, strategies were employed to bring awareness of social and economic issues to the General Conference of The Methodist Episcopal Church in 1908. Herbert Welch and Harry Ward, two MFSS officers, worked with the subcommittee on "The Church and Social Problems," writing much of the report that was approved by the General Conference on May 30, 1908. Within this three-page report was the list of affirmations that composed the original Social Creed—affirmations that became recognized as a Methodist platform on social problems and moved the denomination into a leadership role among churches addressing such questions.

During the autumn of 1908, Frank Mason North, another Federation leader, created a second version of the Social Creed. North was involved in both social activism and ecumenical efforts, and in December 1908, he presented a report to the Federal Council of Churches of Christ in America that included the Methodist document and four additional affirmations regarding rights for workers and abatement of poverty. North lacked any explicit authorization to share the Methodist Social Creed with other denominations, let alone transform the affirmations. However, because of this act, both North and Ward have been designated as original authors of the Social Creed, most likely because of the close proximity of the developments; although during their lifetimes, North received most of the credit since his efforts were more public than Ward's unofficial work with the General Conference subcommittee.

The Social Creed served as a symbol of both ecumenical and social commitment for the Federal Council of Churches. As the revised affirmations were adopted by member denominations, additional changes were often made, threatening the common text. In response the Federal Council of Churches undertook a third revision in 1912 that acknowledged the growing interest in social and economic issues. Two additional declarations were included, and the document was expanded to mention the family, child development, health, liquor traffic, and property.

While deaconesses visited the poor—for the purpose of ministering to their physical and spiritual brokenness—as nurses and domestic visitors, many also functioned in part as students and agents of the new field of quantitative sociology. Deaconesses began to realize that the causes of the depression, sickness, chemical dependency, and despair that they witnessed were not merely the fault of the impoverished themselves but also represented systemic oppression of the immigrant and poor. Their experience challenged older notions that poverty was solely the result of individual depravity. In its later years under the leadership of Isabelle Horton and Winifred Chappell, the deaconess movement worked toward and offered social critique of various efforts addressing social reform in the area of child labor, employment advocacy, temperance, and prostitution.

The sixteen-point Social Creed adopted in 1912 served as the basic pronouncement of the Federal Council of Churches for twenty years, although there were tensions among the member denominations leading to revisions and additions. Additional paragraphs were appended on topics such as community service, industrial conditions, and labor rights. In the years following 1912, a controversy emerged with regard to the language of the creed. Some construed the language as reserved for the ecumenical creeds of Christendom and favored instead the language of social ideals.

The Board of Christian Social Concerns was later formed in 1952 by an amalgamation of various groups to implement the denomination's social creed, reduce duplication of work, and provide a strategic and symbolic presence in Washington, DC, across from the Capitol. Methodists' important work of advocacy for social justice continues based in the same location through the General Board of Church and Society. The United Methodist Church is the only church in the United

States with a physical presence on Capitol Hill. The General Board of Church and Society also maintains a presence at the Church Center for the United Nations in New York City. The General Board of Church and Society provides a persistent voice and strategically works for social justice through advocacy of government policies and allocation of resources. The General Board cares for the Social Principles included in the *Discipline* and *The Book of Resolutions*, both discussed further in the following chapter.

Conclusion

This chapter focuses on the significant impact Methodists make across the world through our mission outreach. The early Methodist movement's strength relied on an ecology of interdependent components, namely small groups for nurturing Christian disciples, preaching and worship settings, and missional outreach in communities. Initially, the Methodists practiced mission among participants of its small groups first in Oxford, Bristol, and then London. As Methodism took root in the United States, mission impact expanded to efforts for racial and gender equality, as well as the establishment of hospitals and institutions of higher education. In the mid-1900s Methodists purchased property across the street from the Capitol in Washington, DC, to house what is now called the General Board of Church and Society. Since its beginnings through the nineteenth and into the twenty-first centuries, Methodists continue to demonstrate the love of God and neighbor in remarkable ways. In the next two chapters, we will reflect on Scripture, the primary text that shapes us as Methodists, and doctrinal materials that assist with the interpretation of Scripture.

CHAPTER 5
TEXTS THAT SHAPE US

The most important text for Christians, including United Methodists, is the Bible. For Wesleyans and Methodists, Scripture is inspired by God and authoritative in the lives of Christian believers. From Scripture we receive all we need to experience God's invitation to salvation in Jesus Christ through the Holy Spirit. Methodist doctrine or beliefs are grounded in Scripture. Scripture shapes our understanding of God's grace for all and teaches us how to grow in God's grace and holiness and share God's grace with others. John Wesley encouraged a belief and practice of "Sola Scriptura," meaning the Bible alone is the inspired Word of God. Wesley, with many other Christians and Methodists, also valued additional doctrinal materials that offer interpretation of the Bible to encourage Christian faith and discipleship. This chapter reflects on the primary role of Scripture in the lives of Methodists as Christian believers, describes resources and practices for its interpretation, and acknowledges doctrinal materials within United Methodism that shape our lives of shared Christian faith.

Primarily Scripture: Reading Scripture with Wesley

John Wesley is often quoted for the emphasis and importance he placed on Scripture in the lives of Christian believers and communities. In Wesley's leadership of the Methodist renewal movement, he wrote and compiled numerous resources, including sermons and commentaries as well as treatises and, with his brother Charles, hymns and worship resources. In the preface to the first volume of John Wesley's sermons, he states:

> O give me the book!...Let me be *homo unius libri* [a person of one book]. Here I am, far from the busy ways of men. I sit down alone: only God is here. In his presence I open, I read his Book; for this end, to find the way to heaven.[1]

John Wesley and Methodists view Scripture as unique. There is no other book or resource in Christian tradition that compares to Scripture. The Holy Bible is a singular book, like no other.

Scripture is unique because God inspired the writing and continues to inspire the reading of Scripture. John Wesley described God's inspiration generally, though inclusive of inspiring Scripture, as the influence of the Holy Spirit to enable persons to love and serve God. The term "inspiration" originates in the Latin from *inspirare*, which means to breathe life into, animate, excite. For John Wesley, God inspired the authors of the many books of the Bible. As Wesley also explained, God inspires and is revealed through individuals and communities as they read Scripture together in worship, study, and devotional settings.

John Wesley never shifts from the prioritization of Scripture, and its inspiration and authority, in the lives of Christians including Methodists. However, Wesley did not read only Scripture. To grow in relationship with God, neighbor, and creation, Wesley read widely and deeply—other books alongside Scripture as well as numerous translations and versions of Scripture. John Wesley argued vehemently against Christians reading only the Bible. Wesley responds with clear opposition to those who claim, "I read only the Bible." Wesley counters, "If you need no book but the Bible, you are got above St. Paul."[2] Instead, he encouraged Christians to seek other sources and resources to read alongside Scripture to deepen and strengthen relationship with God and facilitate sanctification, God's holiness, in believers.

For example, while the Church of England recognized the King James Version as the standard translation used in worship and study, Wesley also studied numerous other versions of the Bible. In addition to reading other English translations of the Bible, he referred to a number of contemporary versions in French and German. However, for Wesley, the Old Testament in Hebrew and the New Testament in Greek were the most valued sources of God's Word. Wesley not only utilized tools for interpretation such as commentaries and concordances but also translation tools such as lexicons. Interestingly, Wesley was not opposed to historical critical methods, though he did not affirm these in isolation. When included among other resources, historical critical methods provide helpful insight into cultural practices of the time and other contextual matters. When read together with other sources and an expectation of God's inspiration and authority, John Wesley understood historical-critical methods to enhance interpretation and discernment of Scripture.

What Is Scripture?

John Wesley and the early Methodists understood that Scripture, while inspired and authoritative, was not always clear and transparent in its meaning and influence on the lives of believers. Our Holy Bible, or Christian Scripture, did not suddenly appear one day from the pen of one author. Scripture is made up of many different genres, or kinds of texts, such as narrative, history, poetry, prophecy, wisdom, and letters. These many kinds of texts were written at different times by diverse authors. John Wesley encouraged believers to explore and study all of Scripture as a means of gaining deeper understanding of God's inspiration through the Bible. Wesley himself seems to have preached on all the books of the Bible, with the exception of only a small number. Wesley prepared numerous resources for Methodists, including a translation and commentary on both the Old and New Testaments: *Explanatory Notes on the New Testament* (1755, with five subsequent editions) and *Notes on the Old Testament* (1765). The former is included among United Methodist doctrinal materials and discussed briefly later in the chapter.

Christian Scripture includes the Old and New Testaments. Simply identifying the books of the Bible can present some complexity. For Protestants, the Bible consists of sixty-six books, twenty-seven in the New Testament and thirty-nine in the Old. This is distinct from the Bible used by Roman Catholics that includes the same twenty-seven New Testament books, but forty-six in the Old Testament. Protestants call these seven additional books the Apocrypha, and Catholics call these the Deuterocanon. The Apocrypha/Deuterocanon is a group of books compiled later than the Hebrew Scriptures or Protestant Old Testament, which shares the same books as Judaism's Hebrew Scripture but in a different order.

The books included in Protestant Christian Scripture were written at different times and places and by different people. Parts of the Old Testament date back approximately three thousand years. The Old Testament's thirty-nine books occur in several sections with multiple types of genres or kinds of writings. Notably, the Old Testament was the Scripture to which Jesus refers. The Torah, or law, or Pentateuch, meaning the first five books of the Old Testament, is the oldest. It was most likely written during the Babylonian exile from the sixth to the fifth centuries BCE. The Old Testament also includes History, Wisdom, and Prophetic books. It's important to recognize that the historical content of the Bible is not written with the same expectations as contemporary history with regard to accuracy and consistency. While full of truth, the historical narrative conveys significant themes pertinent to the time and context. Wisdom books such as Psalms and Proverbs include poetry and lyrics that express deep and varied emotions. Prophetic books provide insightful perspectives from major and minor prophets in distinctive times and circumstances.

The books of the New Testament date from the middle to the end of the first century. This means none of the books of the Bible were written during Jesus Christ's life and ministry, though some (the Gospels and Acts) rely on firsthand verbal accounts. The New Testament's twenty-seven books may be described in three categories: the Gospels, the Pauline Epistles, and the General Epistles, though Acts and Revelation remain distinctive. Significantly, while the Gospels and Epistles of the New Testament date individually to the first century, they do not appear as a composite list until the fourth century. The first known complete list of the New Testament's twenty-seven books appears in a letter written by Athanasius, a bishop of Alexandria, in 367. The New Testament is then canonized, or recognized as Scripture, through church councils dating as early as 382 in Rome, though most likely at Hippo and Carthage in North Africa by 405.

Beginning with God

Methodist doctrines, or beliefs, find their starting place in God—and God's love for all. This may seem an obvious point, beginning with God, but let's reflect for a moment on this, the alternatives, and the implications.

When we begin with God, a theological starting place, we resonate with the overall purpose and main theme of Scripture. How does the Book of Genesis, which means beginning, begin? "When God began to create the heavens and the earth" (Genesis 1:1). Scripture begins with God and God's action of creating everything. When we begin with alternative starting places—for example our own experience, our purpose, our questions, or simply ourselves, an anthropological starting place—our view, perspective, and imagination actually limit us. Our human experience certainly intersects with Scripture. Indeed, Scripture features human experience, first in relationship to God and then to one another and to creation. After all, God created the heavens and the earth, as well as each of us. However, when we begin with anyone—or anything—that is not God, we miss essential attributes, plot twists, and truths contained and implied within Scripture, which was written with God as the main character. Scripture is about God and God's relationship with all creation.

Methodists are skilled at reading Scripture. A central component of Methodist practice, dating to John and Charles Wesley as they searched for faith and vocation, is gathering in small groups for Bible study. We participate in Sunday worship in which sermons are preached from biblical texts often shared across Christian traditions in the lectionary. We even sing hymns, many written by Charles Wesley, that prominently feature scriptural themes. However, in our practices of reading Scripture we sometimes overlook the main theme of the Bible in favor of the granular details of particular passages. Remember your first book report? The assignment most likely included naming the characters, setting, and plot, and often the requirement was to describe the plot in one sentence. In other words, name the main theme. When I encounter Christians, even the most spiritually mature and wise, I find that it can be difficult for us to describe the main overarching theme of Scripture—its main characters, setting, and plot.

When we begin with
God, a theological
starting place,
we resonate with the
overall purpose
and main theme
of Scripture.

Let's attempt a Holy book report. Scripture, or the Bible, is about God. God is the main character in every story and passage, whether mentioned or not. Scripture begins and ends with God and God's activities from Genesis to Revelation. Not only is Scripture primarily about God, but the Bible is a narrative about God's unconditional love for us and our invitation into relationship with God and one another. The story, or salvation narrative, of Scripture includes many twists and turns as well as diverse genres of texts, but the main theme of Scripture in a word is grace, God's grace for all.

A Wesleyan Way
of Reading Scripture

Reading Scripture within the Wesleyan tradition guides us in identifying and emphasizing aspects of the Bible that are crucial for Christian formation and discipleship. John Wesley's reverence for Scripture is clear from his teachings and writings, and those writings help us see Wesley's specific emphases in reading and interpreting the Bible. In one of his essays, Randy Maddox examines Wesley's motivation, purpose, and priorities related to the Bible.[3] Select themes from the essay provide a helpful framework for a Wesleyan reading of Scripture.

A Wesleyan reading of Scripture draws on three central components: (1) *Inspiration of the Holy Spirit*; (2) *Reading in Community*; and (3) *Salvation*. John Wesley consistently referred to and implemented the significance of the *Inspiration of the Holy Spirit* related to Scripture on the authors who composed the Bible, and also for those reading and seeking its guidance. For Wesley, the *Inspiration of the Holy Spirit* is the Holy Spirit's influence on persons, which enables them to love and serve God. When reading Scripture, Wesley also emphasized the importance of *Reading in Community* with others both past and present. Christians should seek one another out for Christian conferencing or holy conversation to help us build up our faith and hone our interpretation of the Bible. Wesley also valued the wisdom those who taught and practiced the Christian faith in earlier generations, which is found in the writings of Christian tradition. Each of these components then contributes to the main purpose or *telos* of John Wesley's reading of Scripture: *Salvation*. Salvation for John Wesley is a present and active reality that brings together belief with practice—that is, an understanding of doctrine with life as a disciple of Jesus Christ. According to Wesley in his sermon "Scripture Way of Salvation," his most mature doctrinal exposition, he states, "It is easily discerned, that these two little words, I mean faith and salvation, include the substance of all the Bible, the marrow, as it were, of the whole Scripture."

John Wesley consistently emphasized the importance of seeking the Spirit's guidance when reading Scripture. Quoting Thomas à Kempis, Wesley encouraged, "We need the same spirit to *understand* the Scripture which enabled the holy [ones] of old to *write* it." Inspiration of the Holy Spirit was important to Wesley for its role in bringing conceptual clarity and understanding. However, while this clarity was a vital aspect of reading Scripture, Wesley's primary commitment was for the reader to personally embrace the saving truth of Scripture—which is a divine gift. While the inspiration of the Holy Spirit enables persons to love and serve God, our response to God's inspiration of Scripture enables our participation in offering salvation and forming believers as disciples in ecclesial communities.

When emphasizing the importance of reading Scripture in community, Wesley recommended "consult[ing] those who are experienced in the things of God, and then the writings whereby, being dead, they yet speak."[4] His emphasis upon those mature in the faith in one's present context as well as the written legacy of those from Christian tradition did not favor solely the scholarly, though this was not dismissed, but rather seasoned Christian character. Wesley acknowledged the deep limitations of all human understanding and the need for society, or community, to cultivate holiness.[5] In his sermon "Upon Our Lord's Sermon on the Mount, 4," he urged, as he consistently did, that true spiritual formation could not occur "without society—without living and conversing with [others]." Wesley also insisted that Scripture should be read both for its understanding and for its practice.[6] A Christian is not one who gives mental assent to specific intellectual ideas, but one who lives and practices their faith alongside and in relationship with others.

For Wesley, the *telos* of the early Methodist movement, and the church, is Salvation: God's gift to creation through the universal atonement of Jesus Christ. In an earlier chapter we discussed the importance of prevenient, justifying, and sanctifying grace in Wesley's understanding of salvation. One aspect of sanctifying grace is our participation in the means of grace, specifically works of piety and mercy, which happens most often in communities of faith. A Wesleyan reading of Scripture places salvation at the center and recognizes the role of the human response to God's gift of salvation taking place in community.

To encourage Methodists to understand Scripture and live faithfully as Christian disciples, John Wesley, and Methodist leaders since, preserve doctrinal materials. In the following pages we will explore several resources that help us interpret the Bible and understand our beliefs within The United Methodist Church and their roles.

What We Believe

Before we explore specific United Methodist doctrinal materials from different times and places, the following section describes significant Christian beliefs that United Methodists share with other Christians. These beliefs, grounded in Scripture and dating to the time of Jesus Christ, are held by Christians and described in the creeds of the early church such as the Apostles' Creed and Nicene Creed. While different denominations may explore different emphases and choose to highlight different aspects, the worldwide family of Christians holds these beliefs.

God is Triune. The Scriptures describe God in three persons, though of one substance: God the Creator of all things; Jesus Christ, God's child, who is fully human and fully divine; and the Holy Spirit, who lives in and surrounds us.

Jesus Christ is the Son of God and born of a woman, Mary. Jesus Christ, also called Emmanuel, God with us, is at the same time fully human and fully divine, of the same substance of the Godhead. Jesus in his full humanity lived and ultimately died by crucifixion on a cross. On the third day, Jesus Christ was resurrected and found alive by women followers.

Methodists, with other Protestants, recognize two sacraments based on Jesus's ministry: baptism and the Lord's Supper. Through baptism individuals confess our belief in the Triune God, repent of our sins, and accept God's grace in Jesus Christ through the Holy Spirit, and are initiated into the body of Christ. The church is an earthly embodiment of Christ's body of faithful followers represented in local churches and denominations across the world where the Word of God is preached and sacraments administered. In local communities of faith, Christians gather for worship, hearing the Scriptures read and the gospel of Jesus Christ proclaimed, sharing prayers, singing hymns, and celebrating the Lord's Supper.

With other Christians we understand Jesus Christ inaugurated God's reign or kingdom. While we hope for our local churches and Christian denomination to participate in God's reign, God's unfolding work is not bound only to the church or specific churches, congregations, even buildings. God's reign is both already, and not yet. By our baptisms we are commissioned to participate in God's work by proclaiming the gospel of Jesus Christ in our words and in our lives.

Doctrinal Materials

The following section describes the doctrinal materials of The United Methodist Church. These documents give a perspective on who we are as a Christian community. Our doctrines, all grounded in Scripture, provide the framework through which we understand ourselves and grow as a church sent by the Triune God to love and serve the world.

John Wesley sent the following with Thomas Coke in 1784 to support Francis Asbury and the emerging Methodist movement in the United States: *The Sunday Service of the Methodists*, a hymnal, the Articles of Religion (revised), Catechism, the General Rules, and a selection of John Wesley's sermons as well as his *Explanatory Notes upon the New Testament*. John Wesley drew from materials developed and used in the Church of England—the *Book of Common Prayer*, Catechism, Thirty-Nine Articles of Religion, and the *Book of Homilies*. These materials informed those he compiled for the Methodists in North America and shape later Methodist doctrinal materials, which represent different kinds of resources from ancient articles to rules for small groups, from a confession to collected sermons. Methodist doctrinal materials reflect Methodism's missional character.

Wesley based the teaching of the early Methodist revival in an uncomplicated Christianity grounded in doctrinal materials from the Church of England. Wesley continued to embody a "middle way" between Roman Catholicism and evangelical piety, particularly of the Puritans. Many scholars, including Albert Outler, have described Methodism as an "evangelical Catholicism."

The Articles of Religion are the oldest of the doctrinal materials, representing a connection with the roots of the Church of England from the 1500s. The Articles of Religion offer a description of Christian beliefs rooted in ancient Christian tradition dating to the early church. The Confession of Faith, from The Evangelical United Brethren Church, a predecessor denomination to United Methodism originating in the eighteenth and nineteenth centuries, gives a description of Christian beliefs in creedal form. The General Rules, prepared for the united societies, or small groups, of the early Methodist renewal movement in eighteenth-century Britain, demonstrate the importance placed by the Wesleys on the integration of practices and belief. The General Rules also demonstrate the importance of growing in grace within communities of faithful. Select sermons of John Wesley and his *Notes upon the New Testament* also serve as a resource for United Methodism.

Contemporary Materials

The United Methodist Church provides contemporary statements, specifically the Social Creed, Social Principles, and *The Book of Resolutions*, which describe Methodist commitments and inform the practices and missional service of Methodists in current contexts. The Social Creed, Social Principles, and *The Book of Resolutions* are different in genre and appeared over the last one hundred years or so. For example, the Social Creed was first composed in 1908. The Social Principles with *The Book of Resolutions* appeared as a part of the formation of The United Methodist Church in 1968 and following. *The Book of Resolutions* originated in 1968 and the Social Principles in 1972 as the result of a study commission.

The Social Creed is a statement of basic convictions emerging from ecumenical efforts among American denominations in the first decade of the twentieth century. It informs, but is still distinct from, the Social Principles, which provide a lengthier and more contemporary statement growing from collaboration of partners in the newly formed United Methodist Church in 1968. The Social Principles represent a statement of basic convictions, moral principles, and applications drawing from the Wesleyan/Methodist traditions as well as those of the Evangelical

United Brethren. *The Book of Resolutions* is a compilation of statements adopted by General Conference to represent the denomination's broad commitments—even if sometimes contradictory—to social concerns of the contemporary context.

Methodism is the only tradition among mainline and other Protestant denominations that has consistently used the term "Social Creed." It is also the only tradition that continues to authorize the use of a social creed to the present time. The Social Creed was a relatively late response among Methodists to the disadvantages and needs incurred by the industrial revolution. Methodists in particular did not assume such social responsibility until 1908 with the adoption of the Social Creed. The first Protestant denominations in the United States to respond to oppressive social conditions were Unitarians, Congregationalists, and Episcopalians. The Methodists and Baptists awoke to their social duty later. While clergymen and professors designed the social gospel response to the urban impact, these accounts tend to overlook the contribution of women to the formulation and practice of social outreach. Women often assumed the responsibility for practices that manifest the social awareness of Christian churches during this period.

The Social Principles are the result of a collaborative effort of representative members from the Methodist and Evangelical United Brethren of the newly formed United Methodist Church. The social declarations of these groups were not in conflict and initially both were printed as the new denomination's Social Principles from 1968. A commission to study the Social Principles was appointed later in 1968, guided by Bishop James Thomas. Instead of selecting one or merging the two, a new document was drafted resulting in Social Principles that restate and build upon the denomination's Social Creed. Moreover, the commission set out to prepare Social Principles that could be used in congregational worship as well as in missional service.

Methodism is the
only tradition
among mainline
and other Protestant
denominations
that has consistently
used the term
"Social Creed."

While the Social Principles reflect an American, particularly United States, set of interests and commitments, they are meant to be culturally adaptable, including the permission for central conferences to make revisions. A growing number of General Conference delegates represent a vital and growing United Methodism outside the United States. Though the Social Principles are translated by the General Board of Church and Society into numerous languages, there is a growing sense that the Social Principles and *Book of Resolutions* reflect mainly United Methodist perspectives in the United States.

A relatively recent development related to the Social Principles occurred at the 2012 General Conference. The 2012 General Conference approved legislation proposed in a petition from three European central conferences to implement a process of revision for the Social Principles with the purpose of making them "more succinct, theologically founded and globally relevant." For those in United Methodism within the United States, one of the most familiar—and provocative—Social Principles comments upon human sexuality. To a United Methodist in Mozambique and other regions of Africa, for example, a more prominent debate is polygamy, a topic the Social Principles does not directly address. The Connectional Table, an appointed body with global representation that coordinates mission, ministries, and resources to implement denomination-wide initiatives, developed a plan to facilitate revisions to the Social Principles. The plan included the convening of conversations across the denomination including Africa, Europe, the Philippines, and the United States. Each conversation was led by a panel composed of international representatives from the denomination. These conversations inform a proposal from the Connectional Table to the General Conference in 2024 to revise the Social Principles for a more comprehensive representation of global United Methodism.

The Book of Resolutions, published every four years alongside the *Discipline*, is a collection of statements adopted by General Conference articulating the denomination's commitments to social issues. All legislation approved by the General Conference is found in either the *Discipline* or *The Book of Resolutions*. *The Book of Resolutions*, totaling approximately one thousand pages, in many ways serves as an appendix to the *Discipline*. Prior to initial publication of *The Book of Resolutions* at the creation of The United Methodist Church in 1968, *The Discipline of the Methodist Church* printed all resolutions of any kind in an appendix. *The Book of Resolutions* seeks to expand the Social Principles, which, like the *Discipline*, it also includes, into a contemporary and living document of social commitments for the denomination.

Each resolution is presented to and must be approved by at least 60 percent of that General Conference for inclusion in *The Book of Resolutions*; it represents the compilation of adopted statements from the previous eight years—or three General Conferences. According to the *Discipline*, "Resolutions are official expressions of The United Methodist Church for eight years following their adoption, after which time they shall be deemed to have expired unless readopted." Program boards and agencies carry the responsibility to review resolutions and recommend revisions to the General Conference, though resolutions may be received by any delegates to General Conference. Numerous resolutions, particularly those related to our doctrines, have received continuous renewal since their initial approval and appearance in *The Book of Resolutions*. Resolutions are organized according to their relatedness to the categories of the Social Principles. In addition to a searchable index of key words, Scripture references are also included.

Interestingly, *The Book of Resolutions* can contain seemingly contradictory resolutions. This can occur because of a number of dynamics related to the General Conference's process for adoption resolutions. While resolutions require a 60 percent affirmative vote for inclusion in *The Book of Resolutions*, the resolutions are considered individually and presented by different representatives. Additionally, a particular resolution may be adopted in one General Conference, yet another seemingly contrasting resolution may be adopted at a later General Conference, but within the eight-year window resulting in publication in the same *Book of Resolutions* edition. The possibility for this creative tension demonstrates the ability of United Methodists to love God, and one another, within the body of Christ, and hold different commitments as we learn together in and with the Holy Spirit.

Our Theological Task: Interpreting Scripture to Participate in Service

"Our Theological Task" offers a methodology for interpreting Scripture for the purpose of practicing our beliefs, or doctrine. Methodist beliefs are all grounded in Scripture. As we noted earlier in this chapter, interpreting Scripture requires careful attention. Scripture, which is inspired and authoritative, includes different kinds of writings from different authors and from different time periods. Our Theological Task, as described in *The Book of Discipline*, is a guide for interpreting Scripture to understand our Christian beliefs and practices. This guide is modeled on John Wesley's writings and practices from the early Methodist renewal movement.

At times this guide, called Our Theological Task, is referred to as the "quadrilateral"—a term coined by Albert Outler, a prolific and influential Methodist scholar active in the second half of the twentieth century. The term "quadrilateral" was used during his role as chair of a Theological Study Commission, which, beginning in 1968, was commissioned to compose a doctrinal statement for the new denomination, The United Methodist Church,[7] adopted four years later at General Conference. This term, often with the qualification of Wesleyan—"Wesleyan quadrilateral"—has become a familiar concept within and beyond United Methodism, although its widespread use has led to some confusion and even misunderstanding of Wesley's commitments as well as Outler's intentions. Interestingly, the term did not appear in the final report of the commission.

During the twentieth century, references to Wesley's method for interpreting Scripture to understand Christian belief and practice appear with more frequency. Wesley's method drew on various combinations of *four* components for support in his theological reflections, though Wesley never uses the term "quadrilateral," or any other term, to describe his reflections. The four components, which make up Our Theological Task, are Scripture, tradition, reason, and experience. Wesley referred to two or three of these in an appeal, but there are no known examples of all four components receiving reference in one place.

When understanding—and practicing—"Our Theological Task" for the purpose of understanding Christian belief and practices within Methodism, it is important to remember that Scripture is primary. Scripture—unique, inspired, and authoritative—takes precedence. Therefore, like much of Christianity, United Methodism continues to hold Scripture as inspired, authoritative, and primary, especially since it demonstrates a wholeness of narrative and purpose.

The second component of "Our Theological Task" is stated simply as "tradition." Christians and Methodists look to the earliest Christians as role models for interpreting Scripture and practicing our faith today. The earliest centuries of the Christian church provide sermons and treatises as well as ecumenical creeds, despite the limited resources available beyond Scripture from this period. John Wesley also held in high esteem the early chapters of the Church of England during the Elizabethan period, following its separation from the Roman Catholic Church—a period that produced the Book of Homilies, Book of Common Prayer, and the Articles of Religion.

When considering experience as a resource for interpreting Scripture, it is important to remember each of these components, with Scripture as primary, overlap in their roles. As Scripture is interpreted by Christians in particular eras, experience, both personal and communal, also informs the interpretation of Scripture. Experience, in the Wesleyan tradition, most often refers to Christian experience and is multifaceted, offering an understanding—and experience—of God's grace as described in Scripture as well as tradition. For Wesley, experience may be mediated, but ideally for Christian experience, through one's faith. There are many different kinds of experiences. For Wesley a Christian's experience and relationship with God form a frame through which to interpret Scripture.

Reason, the fourth component articulated in Our Theological Task, reflecting on Christian beliefs and practices, builds upon the previous three components. According to Rebekah Miles, writing about the role of reason, for Wesley "reason could not serve as an independent source of knowledge [since] . . . reason was limited not only by sin, but also by its own nature and role."[8] Miles goes on to explain that reason, for Wesley, does not generate knowledge. Rather, reason "processes data and knowledge that originate in experience. It is a tool, not a source." As the *Discipline* explains, God's revelation and grace "continually surpass the scope of human language and reason."[9] However, we continue to believe that any disciplined theological work calls for the careful use of reason. Reason enables our pursuit of the Christian faith and our living out of the same. Reason among Christian believers is guided by the Holy Spirit and one's participation in God's sanctification to grow in holiness.

These components—tradition, experience, and reason—facilitate our interpretation and study of Scripture for the purpose of understanding and practicing our Christian faith. While each makes a distinctive contribution, they work together to inform and shape our faithful Christian witness as United Methodists. A helpful image is to envision

Scripture as the basis or seat of a stool, with tradition, experience, and reason as legs of the stool.

Catholic Spirit:
Believing Deeply and Loving Well

United Methodists continue to embody John Wesley's "catholic spirit" as we believe deeply and love well. John Wesley wrote the much-referred-to sermon "Catholic Spirit" in 1750. Admittedly, many references to Wesley's sermon misunderstand the purpose and substance of the sermon by prioritizing a kind of least common denominator doctrinal agreement in favor of loving one another. However, this misses John Wesley's point—and the distinctiveness of United Methodism's continuing "catholic spirit."

Catholic spirit, according to John Wesley—and I assert also for current-day United Methodists—is more nuanced than a broad acceptance of all beliefs. Catholic spirit describes a careful and creative tension between two often-opposing dynamics, believing deeply and loving well. The introduction to Wesley's sermon urges its readers to love well in the midst of deep disagreement regarding belief:

> But although a difference in opinions or modes of worship may prevent an entire external union, yet need it prevent our union in affection? Though we can't think alike, may we not love alike? May we not be of one heart, though we are not of one opinion? Without all doubt we may. Herein all the children of God may unite, notwithstanding these smaller differences. These remaining as they are, they may forward one another in love and in good works.

When read closely, the sermon does not advocate for Christians to dilute or soften their beliefs amid disagreements. Instead, Wesley spends considerable space composing questions to facilitate the deep discernment of one's Christian beliefs alongside not only the possibility, but inevitability of disagreement.

Wesley encouraged his readers to hold fast to their beliefs even and especially in the midst of disagreements. Wesley does not mourn the reality of disagreement, but encourages community during real, deeply held, disagreements. Wesley facilitates community in his sermon "Catholic Spirit" by calling his readers to pray for and learn from those with whom we disagree on matters of deeply held Christian beliefs. By actively reaching out to those with whom we disagree, we practice humility and Christian friendship consistent with those deeply held beliefs. In the second part of the sermon, Wesley commends particular practices to demonstrate a catholic spirit. For example, show love through patience and prayer, encourage good works of the other, and love through word and deed.

At our best United Methodists believe deeply by studying Scripture to know the Triune God, receive God's grace in Jesus Christ through the Holy Spirit, and grow in faithful discipleship through missional service. Believing deeply means taking seriously our faith as revealed to us in the Word of God and handed on to us in Christian tradition. Believing deeply also means continuing to learn and seek formation as God's sanctifying grace works to perfect us in love.

At our best United Methodists also love well. Through receiving God's love for us, we are called by our baptism to share God's love in our words and lives with the world. Loving well as Methodists includes loving our proximate neighbors, those near to us, perhaps sitting in the next pew worshipping together. Loving well as Methodists also means participating in God's unfolding work of justice. As we explored in a previous chapter, the Methodist connection provides numerous opportunities to participate in God's unfolding work in our neighborhoods and around the world.

Conclusion

This chapter begins by focusing on the most important text in the lives of Christian believers, Scripture. All other doctrinal materials within Methodism contribute to interpreting Scripture, the unique and inspired Word of God, describing Christian beliefs, and facilitating Christian practice, including discipleship, worship, mission, and service. A significant emphasis for Methodists is the integration of Christian belief with Christian practice and service. In United Methodism and its predecessor traditions and denominations, beliefs shape practice, informing our polity and facilitating our mission. In the next and final chapter, we will reflect on the present and future challenges and opportunities confronting Methodism.

CHAPTER 6
GROWING IN GRACE

"A Methodist is one who has the love of
God shed abroad in [one's] heart."[1]
—John Wesley, *"The Character of a Methodist," 1742*

We began this study of "knowing who we are" as United Methodists with these words from John Wesley, the founder and leader of the Methodist renewal movement. He wrote this statement in response to the questions "Who is a Methodist?" and "What is the mark?" These questions emerged in criticisms of the movement to which Wesley offered his response expounded in a published booklet. Wesley's response describes Methodists' main characteristic as receiving and sharing God's love and grace.

United Methodism, in the spirit of John Wesley's early Methodist renewal movement, continues to grow in grace. Though no person or church in this life can achieve perfection in love, we can go on to perfection, or continually grow in grace. Growing in grace occurs when individuals and communities are open to the Triune God and participate in God's unfolding love and grace in the world. In this final chapter of our study, we will reflect on Methodism's distinctive characteristics of grace extended to all, community in small groups, connection, and mission and opportunities they provide in our current circumstances. Knowing who we are equips us to look with hope at the present and future to participate in God's love.

Growing in Grace: Responding to Challenges

From pandemics to polemics, few are exempt from the current challenges that impact not only individuals, but local congregations, and our communities. Similar to the context in which the early Methodist renewal movement emerged, we face significant challenges of social conflict, isolation, loneliness, and deep systemic problems such as poverty, racism, and violence. To compound the difficulties, reliable strategies and techniques no longer address the complexities faced. So, what can we do?

Like the challenges faced, one tendency is to accumulate or "learn" more and more complicated techniques. However, another is to simplify. In Matthew, a Pharisee asked Jesus a question, to test him,

> *"Teacher, which commandment in the law is the greatest?" He said to him,*
> *"'You shall love the Lord your God with all your heart and with all your soul*
> *and with all your mind.' This is the greatest and first commandment. And*
> *a second is like it: 'You shall love your neighbor as yourself.' On these two*
> *commandments hang all the Law and the Prophets."*
>
> *(Matthew 22:34-40)*

In these verses, Jesus offers a distilled, simplified version of the Ten Commandments that offer guidance to the covenant people: love God and love neighbors. The life and ministry of Jesus Christ does not negate the significance of the covenant, which includes extensive details, but provides a focus from them, encouraging our love of God and neighbor.

As John Wesley taught and led the early Methodists, the Triune God continues to change the lives of countless people through receiving and sharing the grace of the Triune God, Father, Son, and Holy Spirit. This grace is not merely focused on the inner spiritual well-being of individuals. It envisions the well-being of entire communities and ultimately the world. God's grace found and shared in Methodism is scripturally grounded and reinvigorates the imagination of individuals to transform communities to participate in God's work in the world. United Methodism benefits from the example of early Methodism's carefully balanced ecology of small groups, preaching and worship, and mission.

By reading Scripture carefully and canonically, meaning as a whole story, John Wesley laid the foundations to support a simple, practical, generative movement that received and shared God's salvation and grace extended to all. Through Wesley's writing, teaching, and preaching a distinctive scriptural imagination developed that holds together salvation of souls, bodies, and communities. This imagination fueled the simple practical responsiveness of the Methodist movement to the Holy Spirit. Through studying Scripture, consistent prayer, and practices of love of God and neighbor, Methodism followed the Holy Spirit to facilitate the spiritual renewal of persons and to build structures to respond to the deep needs of society.

How does this translate into navigating the complexities of current challenges? We may need to let go of our vision of how we expect things to be, and in the spirit of early Methodism's holy tenacity experiment to learn from God's unfolding vision. Facilitating ministries in the mildest of challenges takes considerable effort. Navigating during significant challenges takes even more commitment, energy, and focus. Sustaining the energy to follow God's call depends upon relationships in community with the Triune God and one another, like those embodied by early Methodism. Focusing upon God's call in Jesus Christ's commandment to love God and neighbor offers a frame within which to experiment and learn about ministry sustained by the Holy Spirit.

In the following sections we reflect upon three pressing challenges—conflict, isolation and loneliness, and social needs—and Methodism's contributions. Methodism continues to demonstrate the capacity to respond meaningfully to contemporary challenges through our carefully balanced ecology of grace extended to all, community through small groups, connection, as well as mission.

From Conflict to Community

Ironically, one of the things on which most can agree is the presence of deep conflict within our communities. According to a recent Pew Research Center report, the United States stands out among seventeen advanced economies as one of the most conflicted when it comes to questions of social unity. A large majority of persons living in the United States say there are strong political and strong racial and ethnic conflicts in the United States. While US residents are not alone in this regard (France and South Korea also stand out as strongly conflicted), findings from a Pew Research Center report reveal how the United States is more divided than other societies surveyed.[2]

Undergirding the smoldering fires of conflict is a default to the individual, or even a small group of individuals, rather than our identities as baptized children of God and members of the body of Christ. Protestant Christianity in the United States defaults to the individual. Our heritage of revivalism and democracy contributes to this self-understanding. When we think of grace, faith, discipleship, vocation, and leadership, it is most often as individuals. However, throughout Scripture, its readers as children of God are encouraged to identify with the *community* of faithful, whether through covenant in the Old Testament or baptism in the New Testament.

Paul calls us to see ourselves as Christians living in community. From Romans 12:1-2:

> I appeal to you therefore, brothers and sisters, on the basis of God's mercy, to present your bodies as a living sacrifice, holy and acceptable to God, which is your reasonable act of worship. Do not be conformed to this age, but be transformed by the renewing of your minds, so that you may discern what is the will of God—what is good and acceptable and perfect.

John Wesley comments on Romans 12:2 in his *Explanatory Notes on the New Testament*, "*And be not conformed*—Neither in judgment, spirit, nor behaviour; *to this world*—Which, neglecting the will of God, entirely follows its own."[3] Early Methodists faced similar challenges.

What can we learn from these verses? We can learn at least two things: (1) God does not just call an individual, but bodies and minds—our whole selves together, plural. God calls us into community with God and one another. (2) Another important aspect is the emphasis on the renewing of our minds. Our faithfulness is spiritual and physical as well as intellectual. According to Paul in Romans, God calls us into community to learn together how to participate in God's unfolding grace.

Like the circumstances of early Methodism, our United States context suffers from conflict between opposing worldviews, including deeply divided politics as well as religious beliefs. As we discussed in chapter 2, John Wesley navigated a via media or middle way, not compromising between opposing views, but recognizing the truth in each side. By distilling the truth of opposing views both inspired by Scripture, Wesley and the early Methodists embodied a catholic spirit informed by God's grace. Wesley and early Methodists sought to learn from one another in and beyond small group gatherings focused on practicing love of God and neighbor.

Methodism embraces
this call to share
life and faith in
community, not
avoiding conflict,
but learning from
one another in and
through conferencing.

The early Methodist movement shifted its strategy in 1748 from prioritizing preaching to include small groups alongside preaching. Preaching in contexts where bands, class meetings, and other religious societies existed proved to be most effective as demonstrated by the experiment initiated in 1745. Wesley and early Methodists sought to learn from one another in and beyond small group gatherings focused on practicing love of God and neighbor.

One of the things about which John Wesley was most proud was the acceptance of anyone into Methodist small groups. When John Wesley writes about his appreciation for Methodist societies, one of the most significant characteristics is how the Methodists were distinguished by their willingness to welcome anyone into the society meetings. Early Methodists are even described as "friends to all." This did not mean Methodists agreed with all, or even always with one another. But they chose to gather in Christian fellowship to learn from one another in the midst of disagreements and differences. Methodism embraces this call to share life and faith in community, not avoiding conflict, but learning from one another in and through conferencing. From our earliest days, Methodists continue to gather in small groups, congregations, and conferences to encourage one another in Christian faith, discipleship, and mission.

From Isolation to Connection

Even before the COVID-19 pandemic, almost one half of United States adults reported experiencing measurable levels of loneliness. While short-term studies describe relative improvements in some areas, the United States faces critically deep and expansive impact to numerous areas of physical health. In May 2023 Surgeon General Dr. Vivek Murthy issued a report describing an epidemic of loneliness and isolation.[4] The report also warns that the physical consequences of poor connection can be devastating, including a 29 percent increased risk of heart disease, a 32 percent increased risk of stroke, and a 50 percent increased risk of developing dementia for older adults. Dr. Murthy's report included several strategies to respond to the pervasive and dramatic impact of loneliness and isolation including cultivating a culture of connection.

United Methodism is uniquely situated to respond in constructive and helpful ways to the epidemic of loneliness and isolation. From our earliest beginnings, Methodism continues to care for the spiritual and physical well-being of individuals and communities. Through small groups and missional outreach, Methodism cares for whole persons in communities confronting the most difficult of systemic complexities while practicing love of God and neighbor.

Today, in the digital age, each of us is confronted with the opportunities and dangers of connecting via online technologies including social media. Dr. Murthy states, "We are living with technology that has profoundly changed how we interact with each other and how we talk to each other." Dr. Murthy continues, "And you can feel lonely even if you have a lot of people around you, because loneliness is about the quality of your connections."

According to the advisory issued in May 2023 by the US Surgeon General, across age groups, people are spending less time with one another in person than two decades ago. The advisory reported that this was most pronounced in young people age fifteen to twenty-four who had 70 percent less social interaction with their friends. Dr. Murthy said that many young people now use social media as a replacement for in-person relationships, and this often meant lower-quality connections. Dr. Murthy adds, "We also know that for some kids, being online has been a way to find community at a time when many of them have not been able to." Dr. Murthy urges, "What we need to protect against, though, are the elements of technology, and social media in particular, that seek to maximize the amount of time that our children are spending online at the expense of their in-person interactions."

Dr. Murthy began his "We Are Made to Connect" college tour on October 25, 2023, at Duke University. During his remarks Dr. Murthy compared use of digital technologies, including social media, with the use of automobiles. Initially cars were connected to high rates of injury and even loss of life, at which point safety measures were introduced. Similar research-backed approaches are needed for social media and screen use among young people.

The United Methodist Church, with its legacy and continued emphasis on high-quality relationships, is poised to help foster much-needed connection and community among people today. From John Wesley's leadership to the current context, Methodists continue to connect through a variety of means. While Methodism's primary connection is through gathering in the physical presence of others in small groups, worship settings, and conferences, Methodists also consistently deploy the technologies of their day. For John Wesley, the founder of Methodism, tireless letter writing and preparing publications guided the movement as itinerant preachers traveled thousands of miles on horseback.

Knowing who we are as United Methodists gives us resources to contribute to increased healthy connections through in-person and digital means. *The early Methodist movement's distinctiveness was not in its innovation, but in a powerfully simple integration of Christian belief and practice, simply loving God and neighbor—together.* Methodism continues to resist a desire for immediate transformation through quick-fix techniques promising immediate results. Early Methodists connected with one another for mutual support and accountability to grow in grace—or holiness of heart—by loving God and neighbor well. John Wesley claimed in his sermon "Upon Our Lord's Sermon on the Mount, 4" that earnest Christian formation would not occur "without society, without living and conversing with [others]."

From Poverty to
Sufficiency and Flourishing

The US poverty rate saw its largest one-year increase in history, 12.4 percent of Americans now live in poverty according to new 2022 data from the US census, an increase from 7.4 percent in 2021. Child poverty also more than doubled in 2022 to 12.4 percent from 5.2 percent the year before. The US poverty level is now $13,590 for individuals and $23,030 for a family of three. The new data shows that 37.9 million people lived in poverty in 2022.[5]

From its beginnings, Methodists continue to participate in God's transformation in communities. While such transformation often refers to God's grace within individuals through holiness or sanctification, Methodists do not stop with the inner spiritual life. As we explored in chapter 4, when Charles and John Wesley gathered with classmates and colleagues in Oxford, they contemplated the impact of the inner spiritual life on their Christian practices and love of neighbor. In chapters 1 and 5 we reflected on Methodism's missional character grounded in our beliefs. In contrast to other Christian traditions, Methodism did not begin with a set of beliefs to be defended. Methodism's missional character was innate from the very beginning. The beliefs grew and developed as layers in response to relationships nurtured in small groups and communities. Through interactions with others and the steady authentic building of relationships Methodism's missional response to social needs continues to grow.

We explored Methodism's legacy of missional impact beginning with works of charity and empowerment in and beyond small groups in early Methodism. John Wesley and early Methodists created initiatives for accessibility to microfinance, health care, and education. Building on a strong economic ethic from John Wesley and the early Methodists,

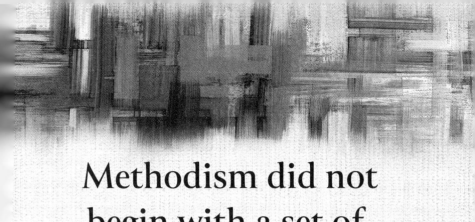

Methodism did not begin with a set of beliefs to be defended. Methodism's missional character was innate from the very beginning. The beliefs grew and developed as layers in response to relationships nurtured in small groups and communities.

Methodists in the United States established numerous hospitals and institutions of higher education. The earliest Methodists resisted slavery, including all in their small groups and ministry. Methodists also affirmed the gifts of women, ordaining the first woman in the United States. While there is always more to learn and ways to grow in God's love and grace, Methodists continue to demonstrate significant advocacy for social justice and response to social needs, such as systemic poverty.

The early Methodist movement's strength relied on an ecology of interdependent components, namely small groups for nurturing Christian disciples, preaching and worship settings, and missional outreach in communities. Initially, Methodists practiced mission among participants of its small groups first in Oxford, Bristol, and then London. As Methodism took root in the United States, mission impact expanded to efforts for racial and gender equality, as well as the establishment of hospitals and institutions of higher education. In the mid-1900s, Methodists purchased property across the street from the Capitol in Washington, DC, to house what is now called the General Board of Church and Society. Since its beginnings through the nineteenth and into the twenty-first centuries Methodists continue to demonstrate the love of God and neighbor in remarkable ways. Today, as mentioned earlier, this heritage continues with United Methodists supporting more than 32 million people in over 1,550 communities across the United States through 52 hospitals and health care systems, 105 community service ministries, and 152 older adult ministries.[6]

Grace *in* the Ashes: Looking Ahead in Hope

United Methodism continues to face a difficult season marked by declining US memberships, disaffiliations by some clergy and congregations, as well as economic pressures. When organizations, even churches, confront serious challenges, internal stresses can erode shared meaning, identity, and purpose. In the following narrative about a very difficult and frightening situation, I invite us to look ahead with hope not despite our circumstances, but in the midst of them.

My family of three was returning home after several days away as we turned onto the long dirt road leading to our place. Our eleven-year-old daughter asked, "Is that smoke in the distance? Is something on fire?" "No, that is probably just dust," I replied. After two months of drought, with daily high temperatures over 100 degrees, the unpaved caliche roads produced great dust plumes visible for miles with every passing vehicle.

As we drew closer, it was clear this was not a dust cloud after all, but smoke from a fire. "Who would burn something when it is so hot and dry?" I thought. Living in a rural setting, residents were more likely to burn debris and rubbish, but most knew better than to do so in such conditions. It turned out that an electrical pole in the field next to our home had thrown a spark, which found a welcome reception in the surrounding parched grass. As the crackling grass ignited, the strong Texas summer winds fed the flames and pushed them swiftly...toward our home. We sped up.

The events that unfolded next, while exciting in themselves, also offer insights related to looking ahead with hope in The United Methodist Church, particularly in this season.

In Times of Crisis: Collaborate

As we quickly drove around the last corner leading to our house, a neighbor was also arriving at our home. It seems the fire started about fifteen minutes before, but already the rising cloud of smoke provided an expansive beacon.

We drove around to the back where a grass fire burned wildly in the pasture and was moving toward our house. Our neighbor followed. All immediately sprang into action. I gathered towels, blankets, and hoses. My husband and our neighbor soaked the towels in water and then used them to put out flames, redirecting them from the house. This was not an approach I would have considered. I was amazed as the wet towels, seemingly so small and ill-equipped for the task, effectively extinguished flames. But the fire was clearly moving faster in all directions than we could control, no matter how many towels were deployed.

Luckily that first neighbor was not the last. A steady stream of neighbors kept coming, and because they were farmers and ranchers, they came prepared. As they would say, "this was not their first rodeo," and they brought all kinds of helpful equipment. But most important were the people themselves, including volunteers from several small fire departments. These were people willing to drop their responsibilities to help in an emergency—people willing to shift their focus to the pressing need, ready to work, and offer comfort and support.

The phrase "many hands make light work" rings true and resonates with the image of the body of Christ (1 Corinthians 12:26). Sharing the burden, with each person using their gifts and skills, suddenly makes impossible tasks possible—and not because smaller parts are divided across a whole. When working together, a shared purpose exponentially creates new possibilities for all. I would have not understood the extent of skills and gifts (and sophisticated equipment) my neighbors could so quickly access had we not faced this crisis.

In The United Methodist Church, we arguably have enjoyed complacency because of our size and relative strength. Confronting difficult challenges together can open a space for us to recognize the skills and gifts God provides across our connection. God seems to specialize in possibilities during times of crisis, inviting God's people to rediscover our dependence upon God and one another.

Wet Blankets Can Actually Be Useful

Often the term "wet blanket" is used in a derogatory manner to describe someone who focuses on problems and/or dulls the excitement. However, wet blankets are remarkably helpful when needing to slow and eventually stop spreading flames.

During a time when some are quick to figuratively burn down institutions because they are not perfect, we need some people willing to slow the flames. For example: checking if claims are accurate before acting on them, practicing interpretive charity in the midst of disagreements, offering constructive counsel for mutual benefits rather than fueling rivalry, and speaking the truth in love. These are all practices of metaphorical wet blankets and contribute constructively to our witness and life together as the body of Christ.

The Least Healthy Substance Burns Longest

The field in which the fire occurred is occupied by a herd of cattle— and cattle leave behind manure. My husband and a dedicated neighbor spent many additional hours until after sunset extinguishing persistent spots of flames. Grass fires are notorious for reigniting long after the initial blaze is quenched, in large part because of the flammability of manure.

We face significant disagreements in the church (as well as insignificant ones), which can be important and helpful. There will be some who hold grudges and subsequently wait for opportunities to reignite conflict. The world is a broken place, and we are all broken people. It is only with God's grace that we can move from unhealthy substances and dangerous fires to become new creations in Jesus Christ through the Holy Spirit.

Again, the image of the body of Christ is instructive. In baptism, when we repent of our sins and accept God's grace, we are initiated into the body of Christ and called to live peacefully with one another. As members of the body of Christ we practice repentance and forgiveness with one another. We are called to receive God's forgiveness while also extending forgiveness to others. In the body of Christ, there may still be fires, but with God's grace we are called and equipped to quench destructive flames.

Uncontrollable Circumstances Are Inevitable

The most difficult aspect of extinguishing the fire was the unpredictability of the wind. We found that if we spread out, and addressed where the fire burned hottest, we could work together to contain the flames.

This is also true in the church. Uncontrollable forces are inevitable, including the powers of sin and death as described by the apostle Paul in Romans. Yet even in the most desperate moments, when fatigue and grief seem to engulf us, God remains in control. God's power and love are sufficient and active. We know how the salvation narrative ends. God's love in Jesus Christ through the Holy Spirit for all creation defeats the powers of sin and death.

God's Grace Always Persists

Through baptism and initiation into the body of Christ we choose to receive and participate in God's love that makes all things new. If the farmers and ranchers helping that day told me once, they told me ten times: the burned land would soon become the most fertile. Just wait. It will be miraculous.

I confess, at the time I was not convinced. My focus was on the present, which seemed quite devastating. The fire was a very frightening and dangerous experience, and one not to be taken lightly. Yet God ultimately managed to work—miraculously—in so many ways that day.

And, months later, the earth left scorched by the fire is the greenest in the field.

Without moving too quickly beyond the experiences of this present season in The United Methodist Church, let us not despair. While we do not wish for disagreements, conflict, suffering, and brokenness, we also know that the Triune God never leaves us or forsakes us. God is always working, making a way, sometimes even miraculous ones. Our role is simply to accept God's love and grace, participating in God's unfolding work by loving God and loving neighbors. In closing, I leave you with this prayer from John Wesley, excerpted from his Covenant Renewal Service first held January 1, 1755. This prayer continues to guide Methodists, usually at the beginning of each year, to rededicate our lives as baptized children of God and members of Jesus Christ's body through the power of the Holy Spirit in and among us.

Covenant Prayer
From John Wesley's Covenant Service, 1780

We are no longer our own, but thine.
Put us to what thou wilt, rank us with whom thou wilt.
Put us to doing, put us to suffering.
Let us be employed by thee or laid aside for thee,
exalted for thee or brought low for thee.
Let us be full, let us be empty.
Let us have all things, let us have nothing.
We freely and heartily yield all things
to thy pleasure and disposal.
And now, O glorious and blessed God,
Father, Son, and Holy Spirit,
thou art ours, and we are thine. So be it.
And the covenant which we have made on earth,
let it be ratified in heaven. Amen.

NOTES

Introduction

1 Rupert Davies, ed., *The Works of John Wesley: The Methodist Societies–History, Nature, and Design* (Nashville: Abingdon Press, 1989), 9:35.

2 W. Reginald Ward and Richard P. Heitzenrater, eds., *The Works of John Wesley: Journals and Diaries I, 1735–1738* (Nashville: Abingdon Press, 1988), 18:612.

Chapter 1

1 Thomas Jackson, ed., *The Works of John Wesley* (London: Wesleyan Conference Office, 1872), 8:299.

2 Davies, *Works*, 9:425.

3 Ward and Heitzenrater, *Works*, 18:249–50.

4 *The Book of Discipline of The United Methodist Church, 2016* (Nashville: The United Methodist Publishing House, 2016), para. 102, 51–52. Used by permission.

Chapter 2

1 Ward and Heitzenrater, *Works*, 18:612.

2 Richard Heitzenrater, *Wesley and the People Called Methodists* (Nashville: Abingdon Press, 1995), 99.

3 Heitzenrater, 100.

4 Heitzenrater, 99–100.

5 *Minutes of the Methodist Conferences: From the first, held in London by the late Rev. John Wesley, A.M., in the year 1744* (London: John Mason, 1862), 23.

6 *Minutes, 1744*, 39.

7 Heitzenrater, 165.

8 Heitzenrater, 181.

9   Heitzenrater, 181, see also map, 180.

10 Still facing occasional persecution, Methodism was considered fanatical by many and not well understood by most. See Heitzenrater, 181.

11 Heitzenrater, 216–17.

12 Heitzenrater, 264–65. See chart.

13 Heitzenrater, 276.

14 See Heitzenrater for more a more detailed description of John's letter to Perronet and the emerging depth and complexities of the movement. Heitzenrater, 179–80.

15 Ward and Heitzenrater, 18:212.

16 Ward and Heitzenrater, 18:212.

17 Davies, II.5, IX.2, X.2, XI.4, 9:254–80.

18 Thomas R. Albin, "An Empirical Study of Early Methodist Spirituality," in *Wesleyan Theology Today: A Bicentennial Theological Consultation*, ed. Theodore Runyon (Nashville: Kingswood Books, 1985), 277. In relation to awakening and conviction, laypeople are mentioned three times more frequently than clergy, twice as often in relation to the new birth, and four times more often in relation to sanctification. Interestingly, in many accounts there is no human catalyst identified. See Albin, 278.

19 Albin, "And Empirical Study of Early Methodist Spirituality," 278.

20 Albin, 278. One individual in the study received such an experience after forty-eight years, creating a mean of two years and four months between conviction and conversion in this study for overall time people participated in society prior to receiving a spiritual experience.

21 *The Book of Discipline, 2016,* para. 104, 77–80. Wesley composed the rules after he expelled sixty-four persons from the Newcastle society in February 1743.

22 *The Book of Discipline, 2016,* para. 104, 78–80.

Chapter 3

1   *The Book of Discipline, 2016,* para. 201, 147.

2   *The Book of Discipline, 2016,* para. 202, 147.

3   *The Book of Discipline, 2016,* para. 216.1.a, 156.

4   *The Book of Discipline, 2016,* para. 217, 157.

5   *The Book of Discipline, 2016,* para. 341.7, 278.

6   *The Book of Discipline, 2016,* para. 215, 155.

7   *The Book of Discipline, 2016,* para. 215, 155.

8   *The Book of Discipline, 2016,* para. 227, 163.

9   *Minutes, 1744,* 215.

10 *The Doctrines and Disciplines of the Methodist Episcopal Church in America with Explanatory Notes by Thomas Coke and Francis Asbury* (Philadelphia: Henry Tuckniss, 1798), 35–36.

11 *The Doctrines and Disciplines*, 35–36.

12 *The Book of Discipline, 2016*, para. 425, 347.

13 *The Book of Discipline, 2016*, para. 425, 347.

14 *The Book of Discipline, 2016*, para. 701, 521.

Chapter 4

1 G. Osborn, ed., *The Poetical Works of John and Charles Wesley: Reprinted from the Originals with the Last Corrections of the Authors; Together with the Poems of Charles Wesley Not Before Published* (London: Wesleyan-Methodist Conference Office, 1868), 1:xxii.

2 "United Methodists At-A-Glance," United Methodist Communications, updated October 13, 2022, https://www.umc.org/en/content/united-methodists-at-a -glance.

3 Randy Maddox, "'Visit the Poor': John Wesley, the Poor, and the Sanctification of Believers," in Richard Heitzenrater, ed., *The Poor and the People Called Methodists* (Nashville: Kingswood Books, 2002), 62.

4 Randy L. Maddox, ed., *The Works of John Wesley: Letters V, 1774–1781* (Nashville: Abingdon Press, 2023), 29:230.

5 Ashley Boggan D., et al., *American Methodism Revised and Updated* (Nashville: Abingdon, 2022), 177–78.

6 Boggan D et al., *American Methodism Revised and Updated*, 174–75.

7 G. Osborn, ed., *The Poetical Works of John and Charles Wesley: Reprinted from the Originals with the Last Corrections of the Authors; Together with the Poems of Charles Wesley Not Before Published* (London: Wesleyan-Methodist Conference Office, 1870), 6:408. Charles Wesley composed the lines for the Kingswood School.

8 Ward and Heitzenrater, 18:612.

9 Charles Elliott, *History of the Great Secession from the Methodist Episcopal Church in the Year 1845, Eventuating in the Organization of the New Church Entitled the "Methodist Episcopal Church South"* (Cincinnati: Swormstedt & Poe for the Methodist Episcopal Church, 1855), 30–31.

Chapter 5

1 Albert C. Outler, ed., *The Works of John Wesley: Sermons I, 1–33* (Nashville: Abingdon Press, 1984), 1:105.

2 *Minutes, 1744*, 68.

3   Randy L. Maddox, "The Rule of Christian Faith, Practice, and Hope: John Wesley on the Bible," *Methodist Review*, Vol. 3 (2011): 1–35.

4   Outler, 1:105–6.

5   Maddox, "The Rule of Christian Faith," 18.

6   Maddox, "The Rule of Christian Faith," 31.

7   In 1968 The Methodist Church and Evangelical United Brethren Church joined together to form a new denomination, The United Methodist Church.

8   Rebekah L. Miles, "The Instrumental Role of Reason," in *Wesley and the Quadrilateral: Renewing the Conversation*, ed. W. Stephen Gunter (Nashville: Abingdon Press, 1997), 77.

9   *The Book of Discipline, 2016*, para. 105, 88.

Chapter 6

1   Davies, 9:35.

2   Aidan Connaughton, "Americans See Stronger Societal Conflicts than People in Other Advanced Economies," Pew Research Center, published October 13, 2021, accessed January 23, 2024, https://www.pewresearch.org/short-reads/2021/10/13/americans-see-stronger-societal-conflicts-than-people-in-other-advanced-economies/.

3   John Wesley, *Explanatory Notes Upon the New Testament* (New York: J. Soule and T. Mason for the Methodist Episcopal Church in the United States, 1818), 409.

4   Juana Summers, Vincent Acovino, and Christopher Intagliata, "America has a loneliness epidemic. Here are 6 steps to address it," *All Things Considered*, published May 2, 2023, https://www.npr.org/2023/05/02/1173418268/loneliness-connection-mental-health-dementia-surgeon-general.

5   Jeremy Ney, "The Surprising Poverty Levels Across the U.S.," *Time*, published October 4, 2023, https://time.com/6320076/american-poverty-levels-state-by-state/.

6   "United Methodists At-A-Glance."

Watch videos based on *Knowing Who We Are: A Wesleyan Way of Grace* with Laceye C. Warner through Amplify Media.

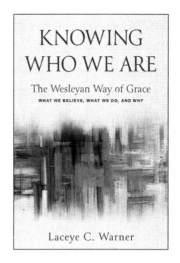

Amplify Media is a multimedia platform that delivers high-quality, searchable content with an emphasis on Wesleyan perspectives for churchwide, group, or individual use on any device at any time. In a world of sometimes overwhelming choices, Amplify gives church leaders and congregants media capabilities that are contemporary, relevant, effective, and, most important, affordable and sustainable.

With *Amplify Media* church leaders can:

- Provide a reliable source of Christian content through a Wesleyan lens for teaching, training, and inspiration in a customizable library
- Deliver their own preaching and worship content in a way the congregation knows and appreciates
- Build the church's capacity to innovate with engaging content and accessible technology
- Equip the congregation to better understand the Bible and its application
- Deepen discipleship beyond the church walls

**Ask your group leader or pastor about Amplify Media
and sign up today at www.AmplifyMedia.com.**